AF539097

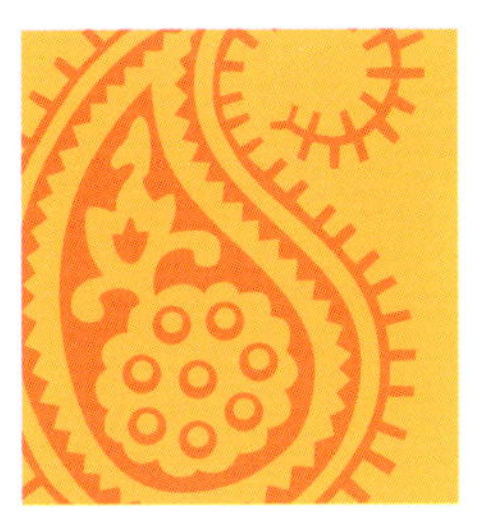

Timeless Traditions Contemporary Forms

Arts and Crafts of Madhya Pradesh

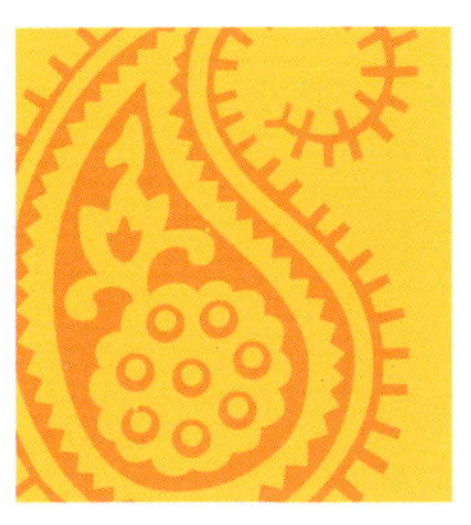

Timeless Traditions Contemporary Forms

Arts and Crafts of Madhya Pradesh

Tinoo Joshi

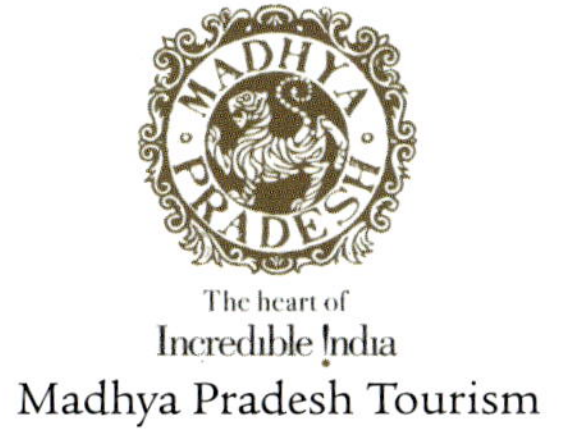

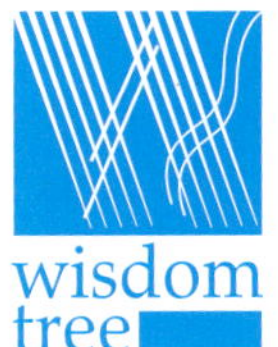

First published in 2010 by
Wisdom Tree
4779/23, Ansari Road, Darya Ganj
New Delhi - 110002
Phone: 91 - 11 - 23247966/ 67/ 68
wisdomtreebooks@gmail.com

The project has been supported by Madhya Pradesh State Tourism Development Corporation Limited.

Printed in India.

ISBN 978-81-8328-159-1

Design: tiffinbox

Selected References

- *Tribal Arts and Crafts of Madhya Pradesh* (*Living Traditions of India*), ed. Shampa Shah, Mapin Publishing Pvt Ltd, Ahmedabad in association with Vanya Prakashan, Bhopal, 1996.
- Chishti, Rita Kapur and Sanyal, Amba, *Saris of India: Madhya Pradesh*, ed. Martand Singh, Wiley Eastern Ltd, Delhi and Amr Vastra Kosh, New Delhi, 1989.
- Census of India, 1961 (Madhya Pradesh). Selected Crafts of Madhya Pradesh: Zari Embroidery and Batwa Making of Bhopal, VIII, Part VII-A, No.1 Delhi: Manager of Publications, 1965.
- Census of India, 1961 (Madhya Pradesh). Textile Dyeing and Hand Printing in Madhya Pradesh, I, Monograph Series, Part VII-A, No.3, Delhi: Manager of Publications, 1970.

Contents

RIGHT
Traditional Gond style of painting on a jewellery box.

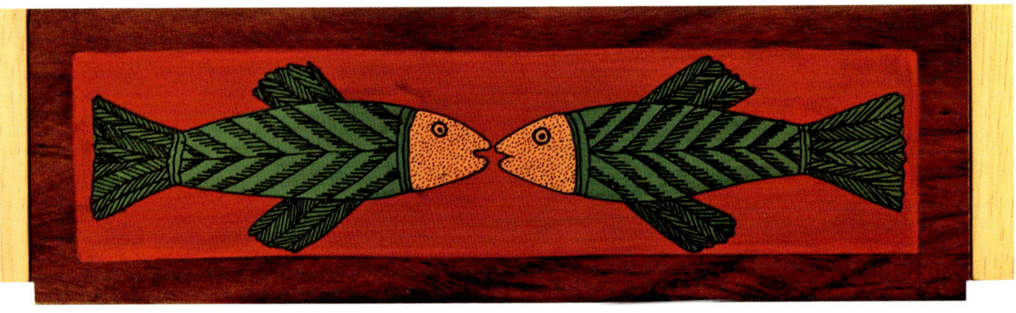

RIGHT
Bagh block printed sari soaking in the Baghini River, a tributary of the Narmada.

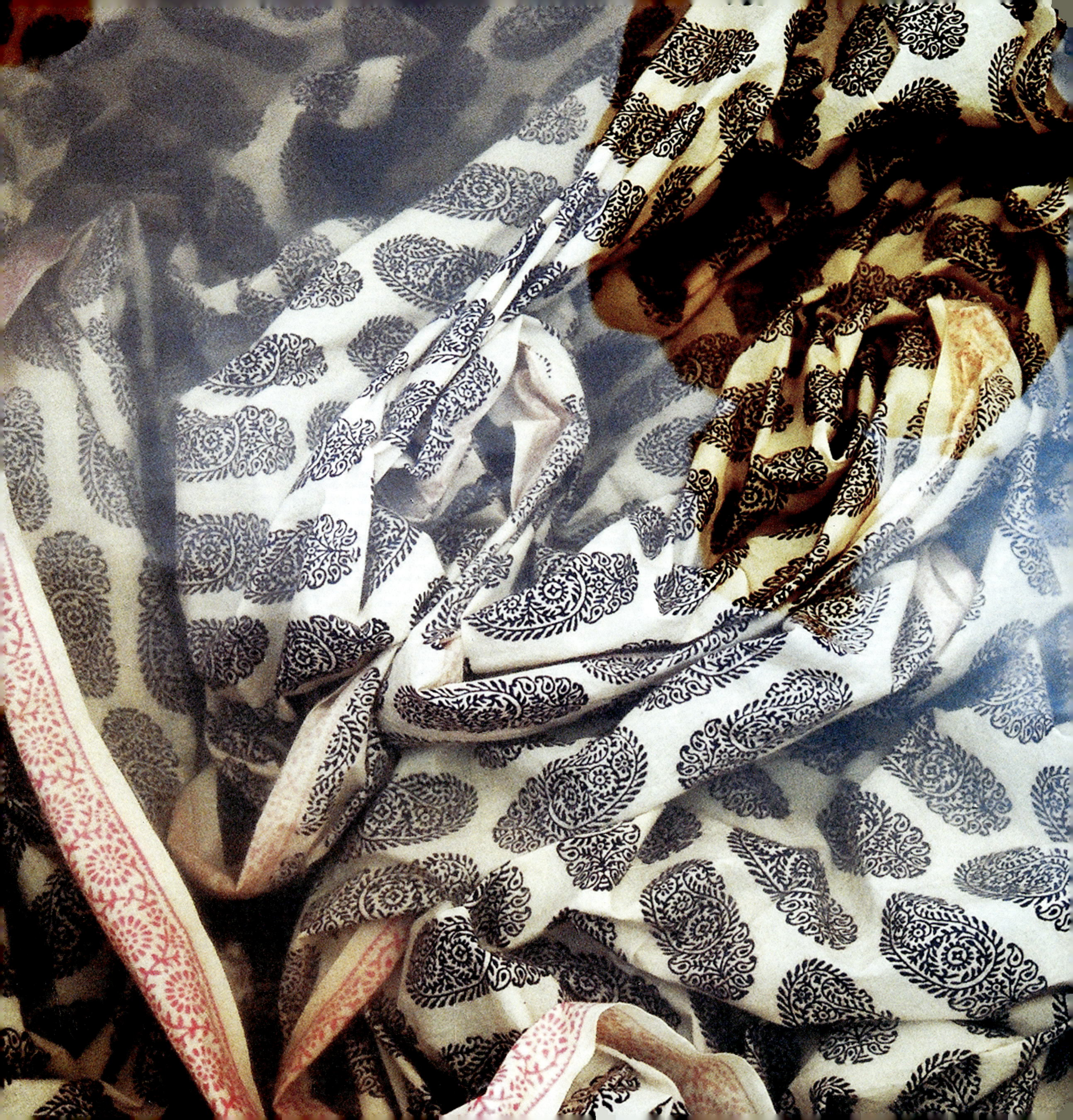

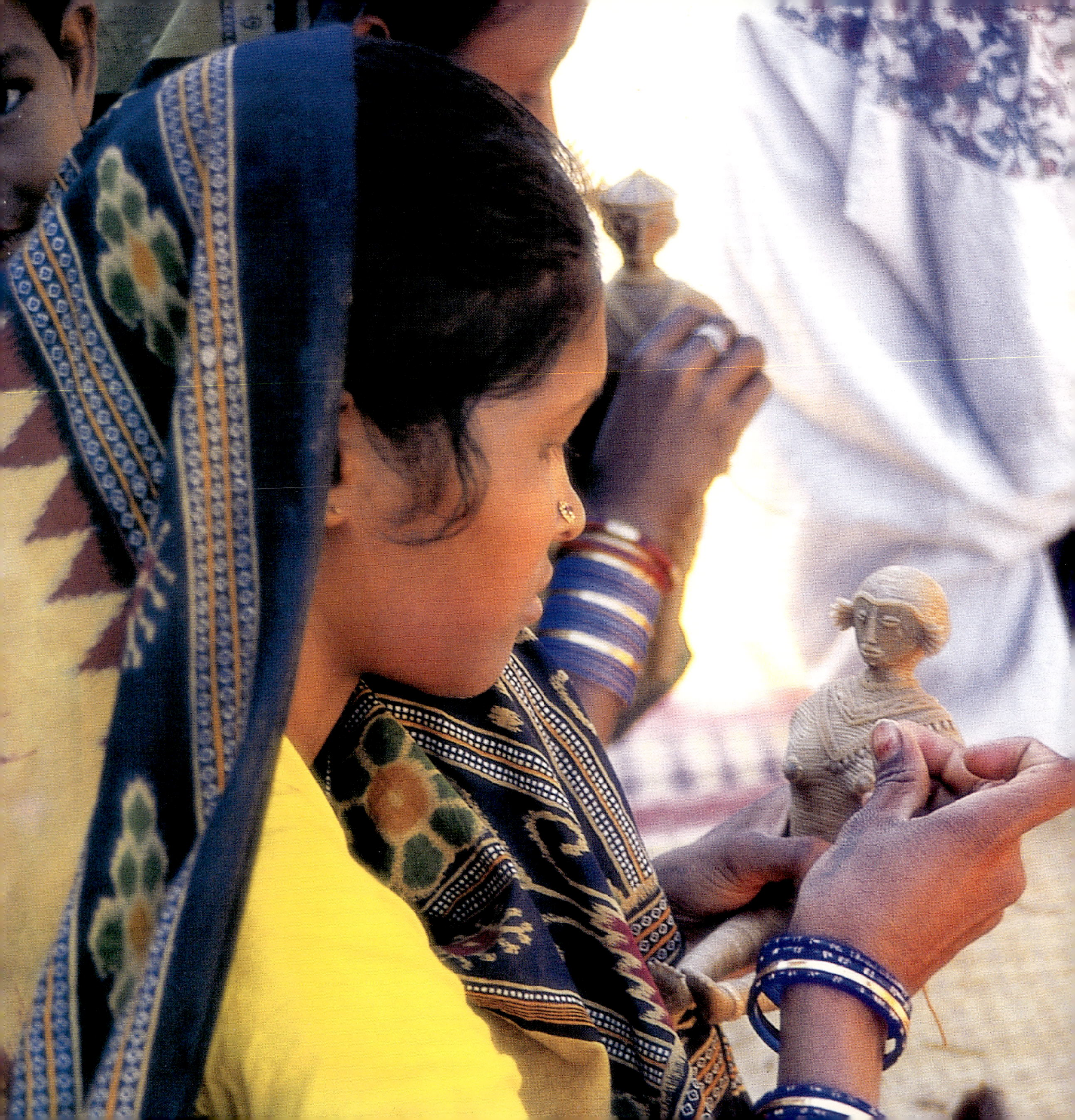

Preface

India's large base of traditional artisans and weavers spread over different states in the country allows for an incredible range and diversity of artistic traditions and heritage. In this modern age, when the definition of a market is fast changing and expanding due to rapidly evolving technological innovations, handmade items are facing stiff competition even in the traditional market place. Given the significance of India's rich cultural heritage, it is worthwhile to undertake a journey to understand how the traditional arts and crafts of Madhya Pradesh have developed over time, what their status is today and what the future holds for these aesthetic creations.

Crafts are a true expression of a community's cultural identity. Traditionally, artisans and weavers used natural and locally available resources combined with their creative skill set and intellect to provide goods and services in many diverse forms. Traditional craft works often depict the social and aesthetic character of a society, and have been sustained over time not only because of their rich symbolic content, be it religious or socio-cultural, but also because of the contribution to the socio-economic growth of the region. The arts and crafts of any region are thus inextricably linked to society as products and sustenance of culture.

LEFT
A Jhara tribal woman making a traditional metal sculpture in Raigarh.

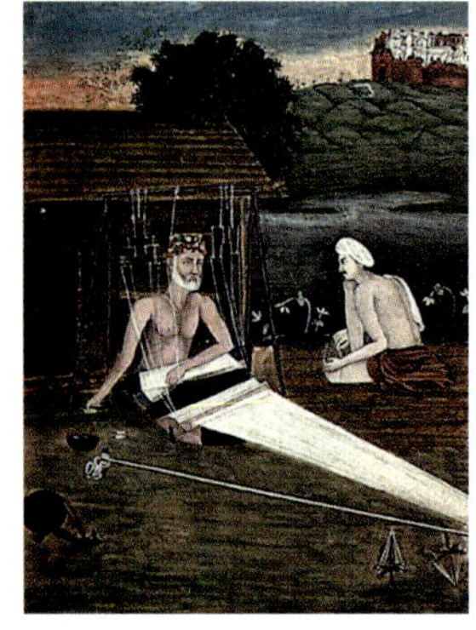

Arts and Crafts Under British Rule

Between 1850 and 1875, the British developed a number of art schools for training Indian artisans under the aegis of the Department of Public Intervention. Lockwood Kipling (1837 - 1911) served as principal of the Mayo School of Arts in Lahore, but he also took a serious interest in stimulating and sustaining traditional Indian skills such as wood carving, furniture making and metal craft. In 1851, the Great Exhibition at London's Crystal Palace included the display of textiles, metal craft, wood craft, jewellery and enamel products, arousing English interest in Indian arts and crafts. In 1883, the Government of India actively sought to encourage arts and crafts, and sponsored the publication of the *Illustrated Journal of Indian Art and Teaching*. In 1886, a Royal Commission was organised. Led by the Prince of Wales, the colonial and Indian exhibit was displayed in London, once again, showcasing the excellence of Indian craftsmanship.

State Intervention

In the post-Independence era, steps were taken to improve the conditions of artisans in India. In the First Five Year Plan (1951), six important boards at an all-India level were set up for the promotion of handicrafts, village and small industries, which continue to nurture and promote the cause for which they were founded. These are:

- Khadi and Village Industries Board

ABOVE
A painting of Kabir at his loom. He was a mystic, a free-thinker and a weaver who lived in Banaras during the fifteenth century.

- The All India Handicrafts Board
- The All India Handloom Board
- The Central Silk Board
- Coir Board
- Small Industries Board

It is interesting to note that in 1961 it was the office of the Registrar General of India which played an instrumental role in initiating the first official documentation process for assessing the number of households in the country traditionally engaged in the work of handloom, handicrafts and allied cottage sector industries.

The Government of Madhya Pradesh had also initiated the process of setting up similar institutions to provide all the necessary patronage required to promote arts and crafts. Various steps were taken to provide incentives for augmenting production, to improve the organisational capacity of this huge informal sector of economy, for training and extension, credit and marketing, including export. These measures have helped this sector to enlarge and consolidate the position that it has so far been enjoying in the nation's economic scenario.

However, the introduction of technology enabling the mechanisation of the production process has lead wider product availability at a relatively lesser price, affecting the status of these products. While on the one hand, it has created an awareness to strengthen and preserve the arts and crafts of India as national heritage, on the other hand, another dimension has

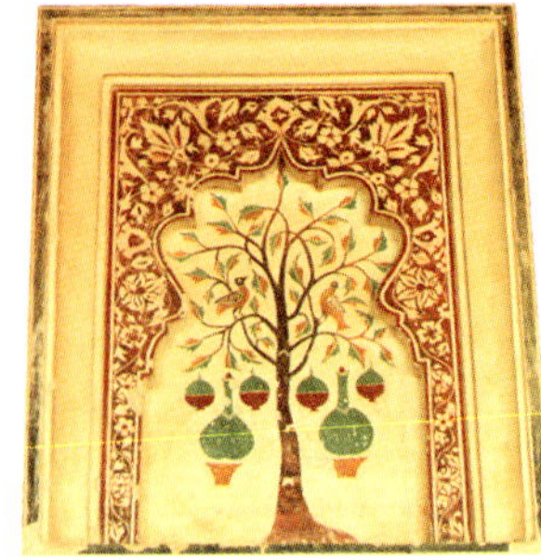

emerged using the traditional skill base of an area or a region as a better known contemporary product line. This is perceived to be more modern and in demand by the urban population in India and is particularly in demand for export purposes, thus helping the country earn foreign exchange. Finally, the advent of a global market economy in the nineties in India was a watershed in the history of the development of arts and crafts. This brought about a paradigm shift in the strategy for further intervention based on both the state and private-public initiative. The evolution of arts and crafts in Madhya Pradesh has to be viewed in this historical perspective. The future dimension has to be measured in terms of how much and what is to be preserved, to what extent state intervention is called for and how the people engaged in it need to be educated and trained in the process of competing in the free market economy.

Defining Artisanal Products

There is no universal definition of artisanal products because of their very nature and diversity. However, a broad definition was adopted during the international symposium organised by the UNESCO/ITC on Crafts and the International Market: Trade and Customs Codification held in Manila, in October, 1977.

ABOVE
A detail of stone inlay work at Datia Fort, a magnificent blend of Rajput and Mughal architecture.

> Artisanal products are those produced by artisans either completely by hand or with the help of hand-tools or even mechanical means, as long as the direct manual contribution of the artisan remains the most substantial

component of the finished product. These are produced without restriction in terms of quantity and using raw materials from sustainable resources. The special nature of artisanal products derives from their distinctive features which can be utilitarian, aesthetic, artistic, creative, culturally attached, decorative, functional, traditional, religiously and socially symbolic and significant.

According to UNESCO, artisanal products can be classified into six broad divisions based on the material used and/or techniques. These are:

- Basket/Wicker/Vegetable fibre works
- Leather
- Metal
- Pottery
- Textiles
- Wood

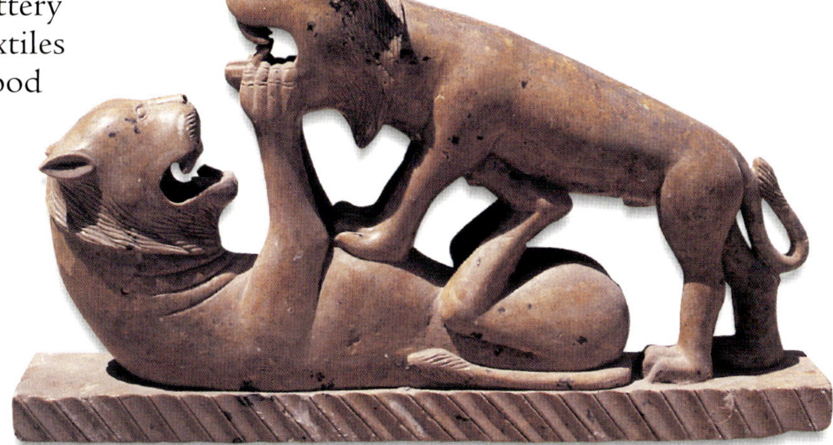

LEFT
Soapstone carving of tigers, a typical stone craft of Tikamgarh.

PAGE 16
Young boys sit outside a temple in Gwalior dedicated to Bhairav, an incarnation of Lord Shiva, depicted in typical chitera *folk art style.*

There is an additional division which includes all those other materials used in the making of crafts according to country, region, etc. For example, stone, glass, bone, horn, shell and mother-of-pearl fall into this category. This also includes other categories like jewellery making, musical instruments, toys and theatre.

Given this context, *Timeless Traditions; Contemporary Forms* attempts to bring out the strong socio-economic and cultural factors that have been the inspiration for the evolution of the rich tradition of arts and crafts in Madhya Pradesh. It also portrays the strong patronage given by the erstwhile rulers of Gwalior, Bhopal, Ujjain, Indore and other regions. These traditions are not bound by any time or reference point as they continue to be timeless heritage products, reminding each passing generation of the great creative mind of their ancestors. It is interesting to note that these creations, even at a time when they were not connected with the outside world, shared similar features in terms of concepts, inspiration and techniques used with crafts made in other parts of India and the world over.

The present and the future for arts and crafts in India throws up immense opportunities, given the strong influence of the multidisciplinary knowledge that has pervaded each field and the interface of design, technology and management which is inseparable. Traditional arts and crafts are important not only because of their heritage value, but also because they have become, over the years, an important means of economic livelihood for a large segment of society. Most importantly, unlike any other product which is born of mechanical technology, arts and crafts will continue to have a high degree of involvement of human emotion and socio-cultural inspiration which truly gives them a unique identity.

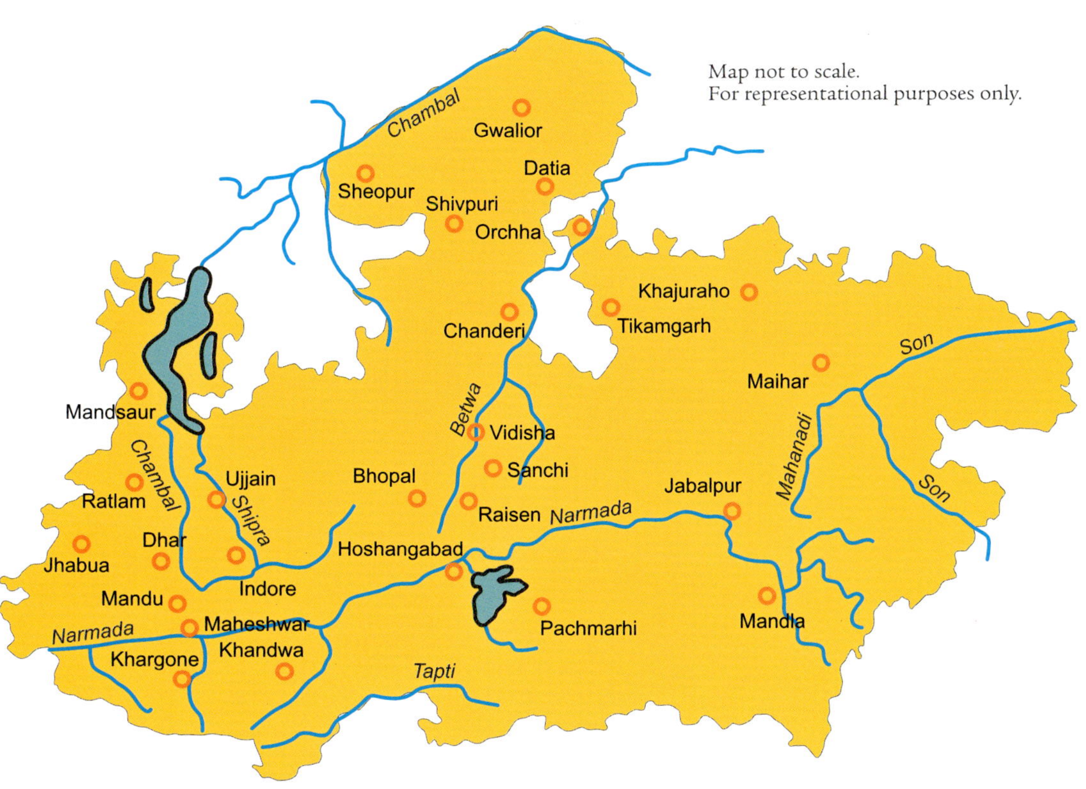

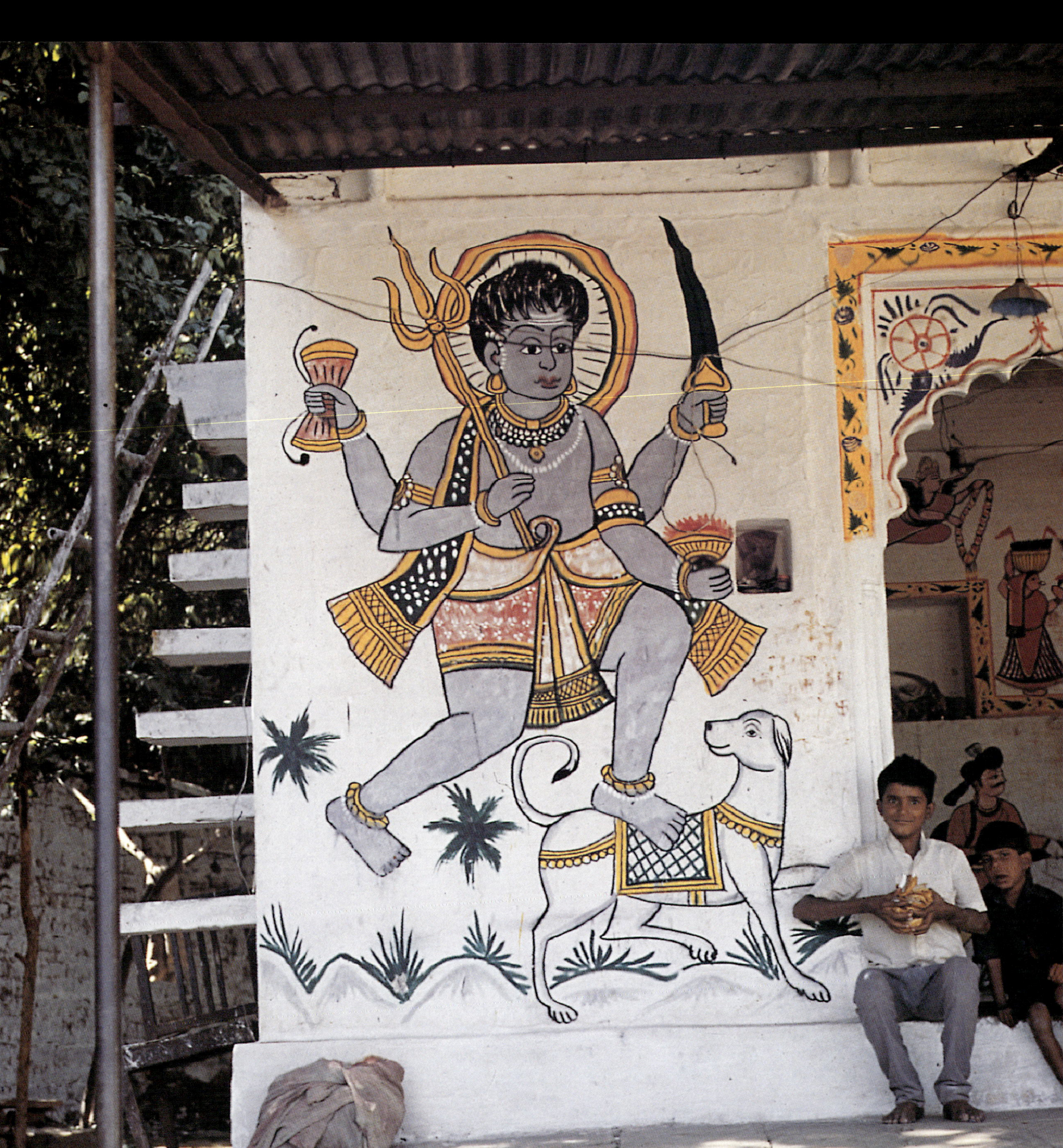

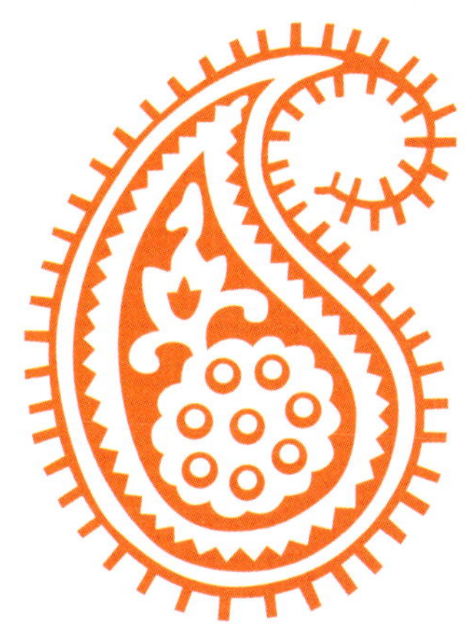

Socio-economic and Cultural Expressions of Arts and Crafts

The Evolution of Arts and Crafts of Madhya Pradesh as Traditional and Heritage Products

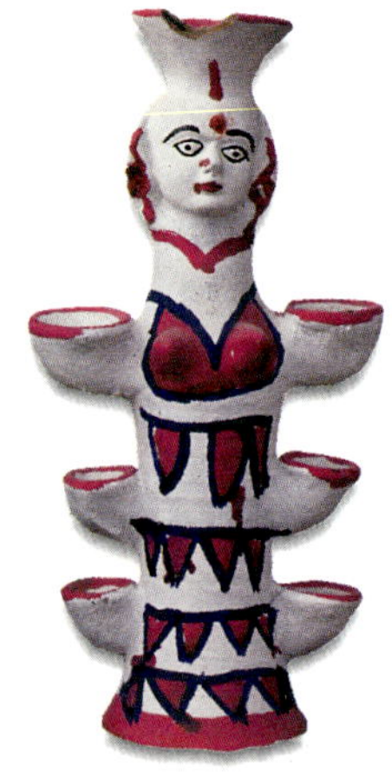

ABOVE
Terracotta painted stand for diyas, *earthen lamps, painted in a typical folk style, Dhar.*

No analysis of any art or craft is complete without understanding and interpreting the origin of various art forms there. This is important, as most of them are closely derived from the established and deep-rooted tradition of folk and religious practises and are generally derived from the dominant indigenous culture and rituals of that particular region.

These traditional art forms continue to be alive in the midst of modern and urban contexts through their use in marriages, festivals and other special occasions in the form of decorations in temples, houses, clothing, etc. These art forms are reflected through motifs and the use of bright colours. The designs and motifs are expressed through different techniques, using as diverse materials as brass, stone, wood, clay relief, wall paintings, paper and textile, among other things. These designs have stood the test of time because they have passed through generations. Many of these are known to have been evolved by gifted tribal craftsmen and women who are sensitive to the concept of beauty.

This traditional excellence also tells us that in each craft form and in each region, generations of craft communities maintain their distinctive style. The village craftspeople – the carpenter, weaver, dyer, potter, bamboo basket maker, wood carver, goldsmith and painter – all have evolved their

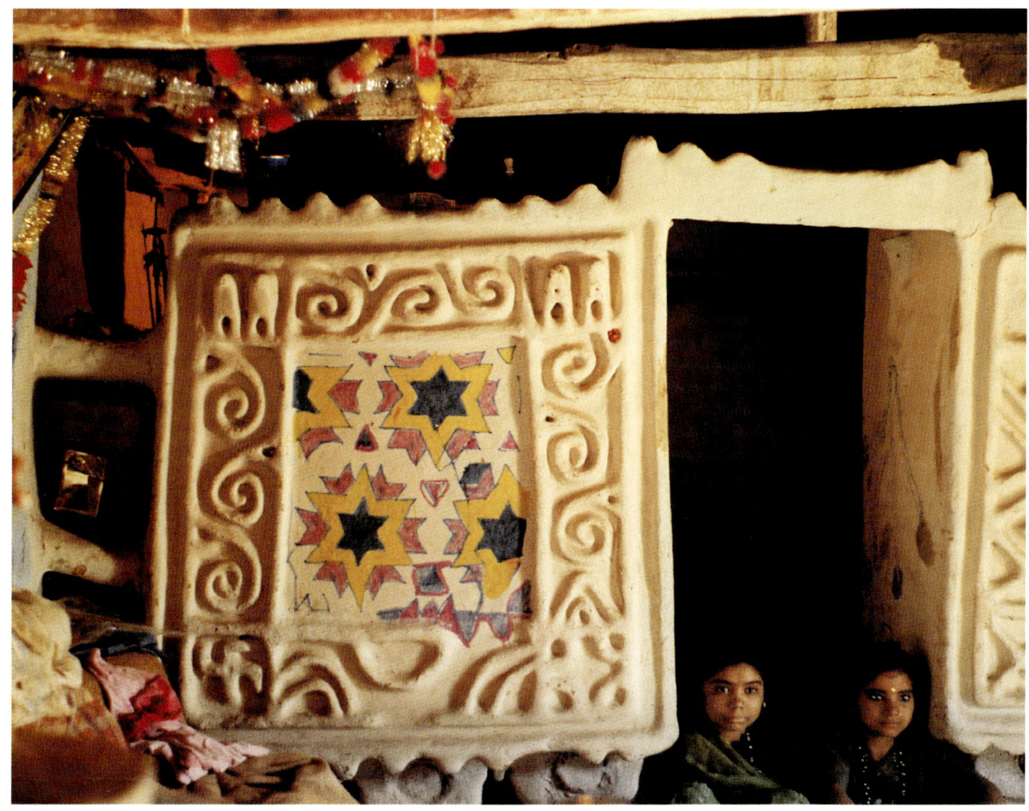

ABOVE
Inside a typical tribal home in Raisen where the walls are commonly sculpted and painted in bright colours.

traditional art forms from sheer societal needs. The journey of this evolution of traditional forms that are practised in different regions by various communities cannot be complete without describing some of the characteristic features that differentiate each art form.

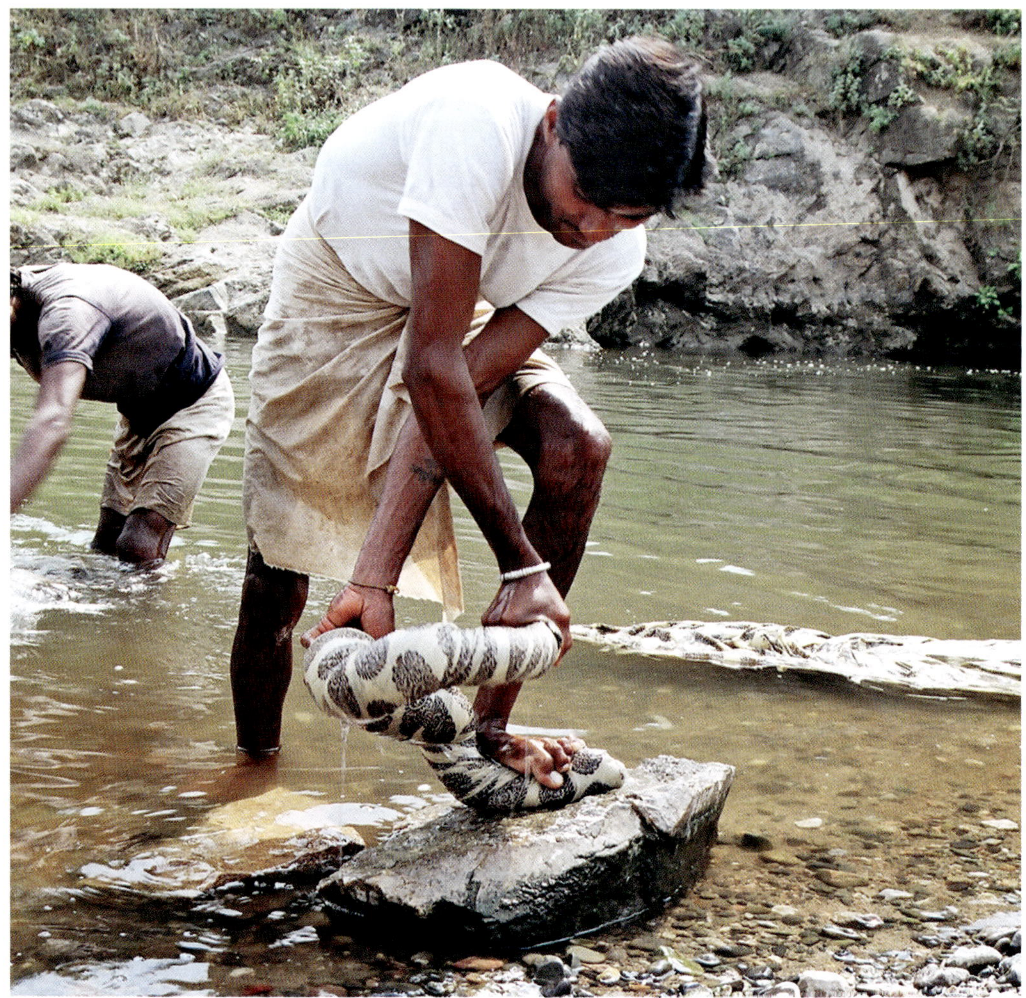

RIGHT
A craftsman wringing out a block printed sari after soaking it in the Baghini River to fix its colours.

Textile Heritage — A Journey Through the Handloom Clusters

Madhya Pradesh is bestowed with a vibrant heritage of handcrafted textiles in the areas of weaving, dyeing and block printing, spread over different parts of the state. Weavers, particularly master weavers, have been instrumental in continuing the rich tradition of weaving with each cluster specialising in a specific kind of weave, dyeing practise, or unique block print. Each cluster is the result of a specific loom technology which has not changed much in terms of configuration which can sometimes work as a disadvantage and sometimes as a traditional strength.

Textiles of Madhya Pradesh have evolved through a process of assimilation and adaptation of techniques from the adjoining states arising out of exchanges taking place through trade routes including the movement of Mughal armies, and the influence of design concepts, the use of raw materials, and skills from far and wide. With the passage of time, these textiles have also seen the development of local skills, and socio-cultural perspectives as reflected through motifs and colours. Chanderi, Maheshwar, Burhanpur, Balaghat, Saunsar, Padana and Sarangpur are prime examples of this process of development. Chanderi is the most important weaving township and has been nurtured by the state government for many years. During the Mughal period, Chanderi cottons were famous and comparisons were made with the fine Dhaka muslins

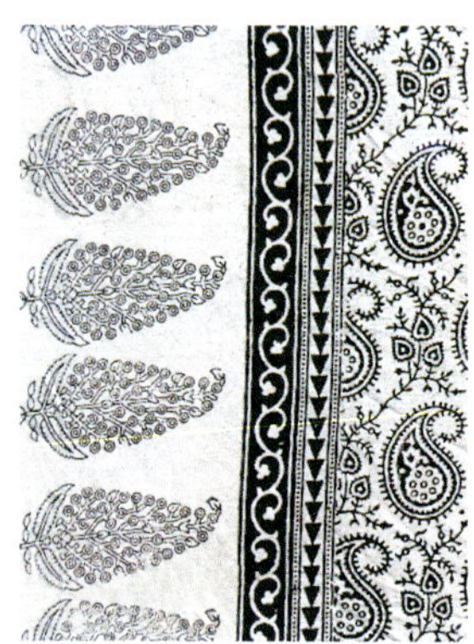

when they could weave in 300 counts of cotton. However, in the thirties, silk came from Calcutta (now Kolkata) through the silk trade route and was introduced as warp with cotton in the weft. The fine cotton traditions are no longer practised because of a lack of market as well as the fact that the local sizing technique is no longer available. The pure cotton sari has become a product of the past and has been replaced by silk or silk warp and cotton weft since the fifties. There is the influence of Maharashtra and Banaras in the *booti* motifs in Chanderi fabrics.

It is through the efforts of Rani Ahilyabai Holkar of Indore that Maheshwar is one of the most significant sari weaving regions of India. It is said that Rani Ahilyabai settled a large number of weavers from Surat in Maheshwar to weave saris for the royal household. Today, in a continuation of this tradition, Maheshwar is famous for Maheshwari saris, which are light and are available in both cotton and cotton-silk, with a significant number of looms being operated by women weavers. Maheshwar, like Chanderi has, in the past, seen woven saris of up to 300 cotton thread count. Maheshwar is well known for its lustrous textiles which use mercerised cotton as well as *zari* borders, and are characterised by rich variations of self stripes and checks on the body. Once silk was introduced in the early forties, its use became very popular in the Maheshwari saris.

ABOVE
A detail of intricate block prints used commonly in saris, bed spreads and other textile products.

Weavers in Pedana and Sarangpur in Rajgarh district were once well known for their finely woven *zari* edged turban cloths referred to as *safa*s and *pagdi*s. Somewhere between 1953 and 1960, they were introduced to

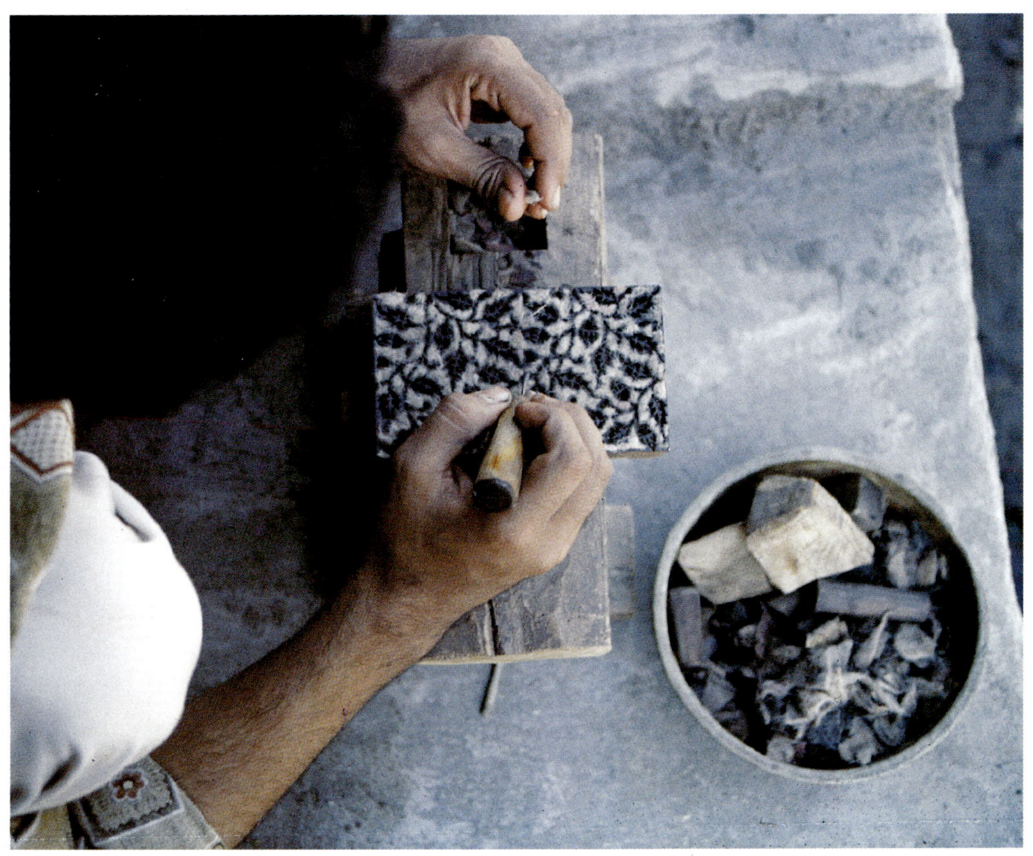

ABOVE
A craftsman preparing a block of wood, which will later be used with vegetable dyes for block printing textiles.

bootidar saris of Indore. In the seventies, they became experts in weaving Kota Masuria saris in 120 counts of cotton-silk. They had the capacity of becoming fine count sari weavers.

Textile Dyeing and Block Printing Hubs in Madhya Pradesh

Two non-structural ornamentation processes involved with textile production are dyeing and printing. Dyeing is an old art, which finds mention even in historical writings. Ancient China is supposed to be the origin of block printing, where it was assumed that earth pigments to paint block prints on textiles were used as far back as 400 BC. This is reported in the archives of a museum in the Forbidden City, Beijing, which has a few wooden blocks dating from 200 BC.

Fragments of coloured cloth and traces of madder dye found in Mohenjodaro and Harappa confirm that dyeing is an ancient Indian art form. It was practised from Vedic times, particularly the use of red and yellow for cloth, as the colours were considered auspicious. Kautilya's *Arthashastra* mentions white, pure red, rose red, and black coloured woollens. Indian dyed cotton was considered important in imperial Rome. Before the fifteenth century, after which sea trade became common place, Indian dyed cottons were quite popular in Europe. Gujarat's cheap resist-dyed cloth was much in demand both in the Middle East and in Malaysia. In the *Ramayana*, there are numerous references to printed cloth. The *Mahabharata* also refers to printed cloth. The secret of dyeing cotton, which was the basis of the printing process, was very slow to spread beyond India and therefore had time to become a specialised craft from region to region.

RIGHT
Bed spreads stretched out to dry in the sun, Bhairongarh.

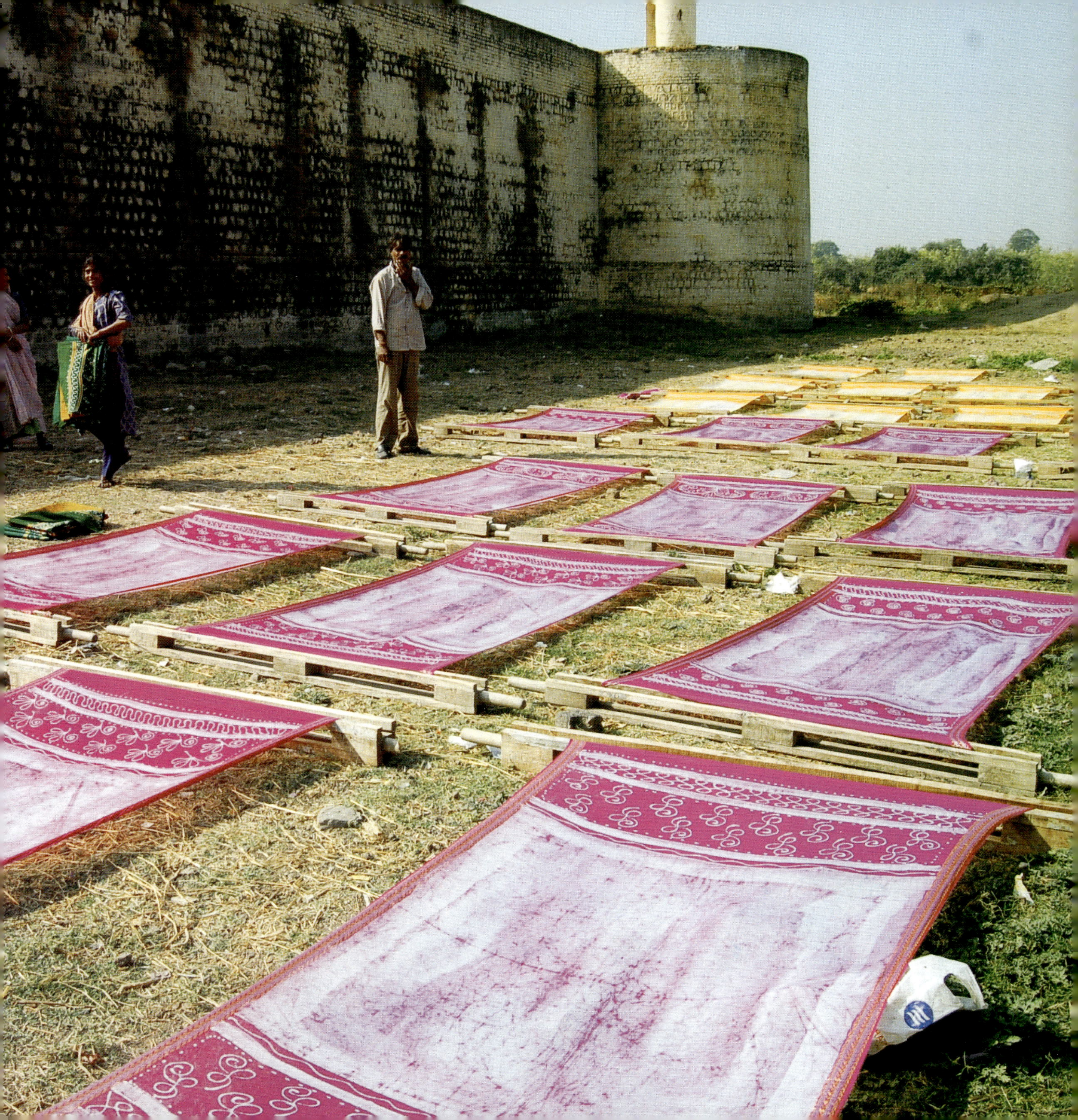

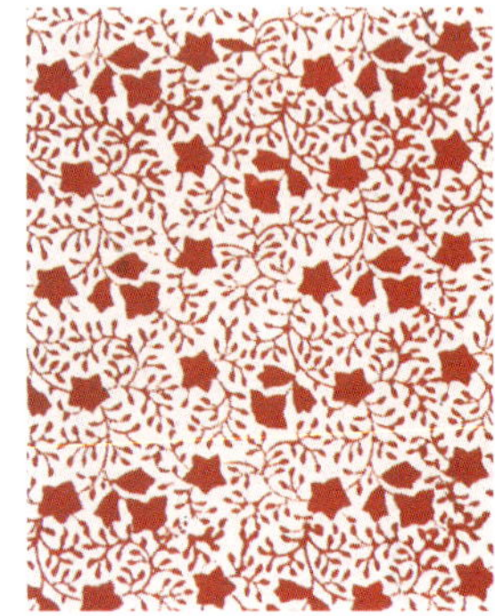

Malwa in Madhya Pradesh and the adjoining regions of Gujarat and Rajasthan have a long history of being very important regions for textile products. Ujjain was and continues to be a centre of coarse-dyed cotton cloth. In this region, different techniques of dyeing and printing are practised side by side. Among them are tie-dyeing, direct dyeing and printing, resist-dyeing and printing, screen printing and *rogan* printing, which involves the use of a thick, bright paste which is painted on single coloured cotton.

Resist-dyeing is the technique in which the fabric is lifted and tied in such a way that one gets spherical shapes. The piece of fabric is then alternately dipped in a dye vat and hung in the air until the colour develops. When the ties have been removed, the pattern emerges in that part of the fabric where the dye has not been able to penetrate.

The important centres of tie-dye work in Madhya Pradesh are Jawad, Tarapur, Ummedpura and Bhairongarh. For resist-dyeing and printing and direct dyeing and printing, important areas are Gwalior, Indore, Mandsaur, Jawad, Tarapur, Ummedpura and Sheopur. Textile dyeing and printing in Madhya Pradesh, as in other states, is practised by professional dyers and printers who have been practising this craft for generations. Three communities are traditionally connected with the craft. They are Chhipa, which includes both Hindus and Muslims, Rangrez and Nilgar.

ABOVE
Detail of a Bagh print.

The most important centre of block printing, Bagh has left an indelible mark in the area of textile block printing in the country. It is characterised by the use of vegetable dyes using only *aal*, or madder root, *babool* bark, *dhawda* flower and indigo for basic red, pink, yellow, blue and black colour range. The colours continue to be vibrant and the technique is practised by a few families only. The marketability continues to be encouraging with Bhairongarh close to a second position. An exceptional printer in Bagh, Ismail Sulaiman Khatri, has managed over the years to sustain a high quality of printing which is being followed by the members of the next generation in his family.

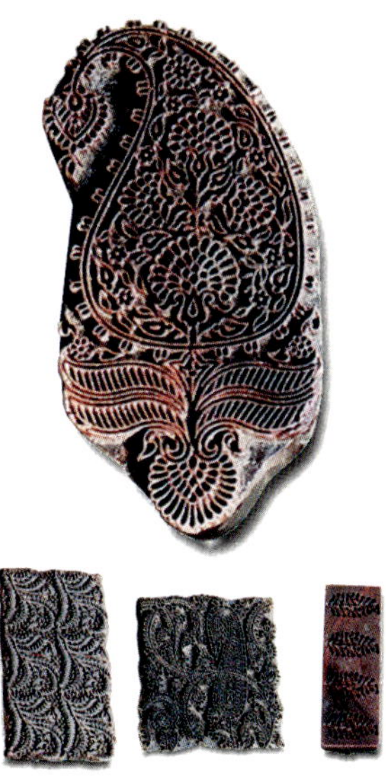

Bhairongarh has been a traditional printing area where the printers came from Rajasthan as the Shipra River provided abundant water with which to wash the cloth and plenty of open space for drying the printed fabric. Traditional colours included madder red, *hirakasi* (a locally grown medicinal herb) black, indigo blue and a wide range of non fast colours.

Craftspeople in Jawad and Ummedpura practised the technique of wax resist-dyeing, used for double sided indigo dyed *nandana* print. The *nandana* motif based on the mango form is worn largely by the tribals or the Mahajan community.

ABOVE
Different kinds of carved wooden blocks used for printing.

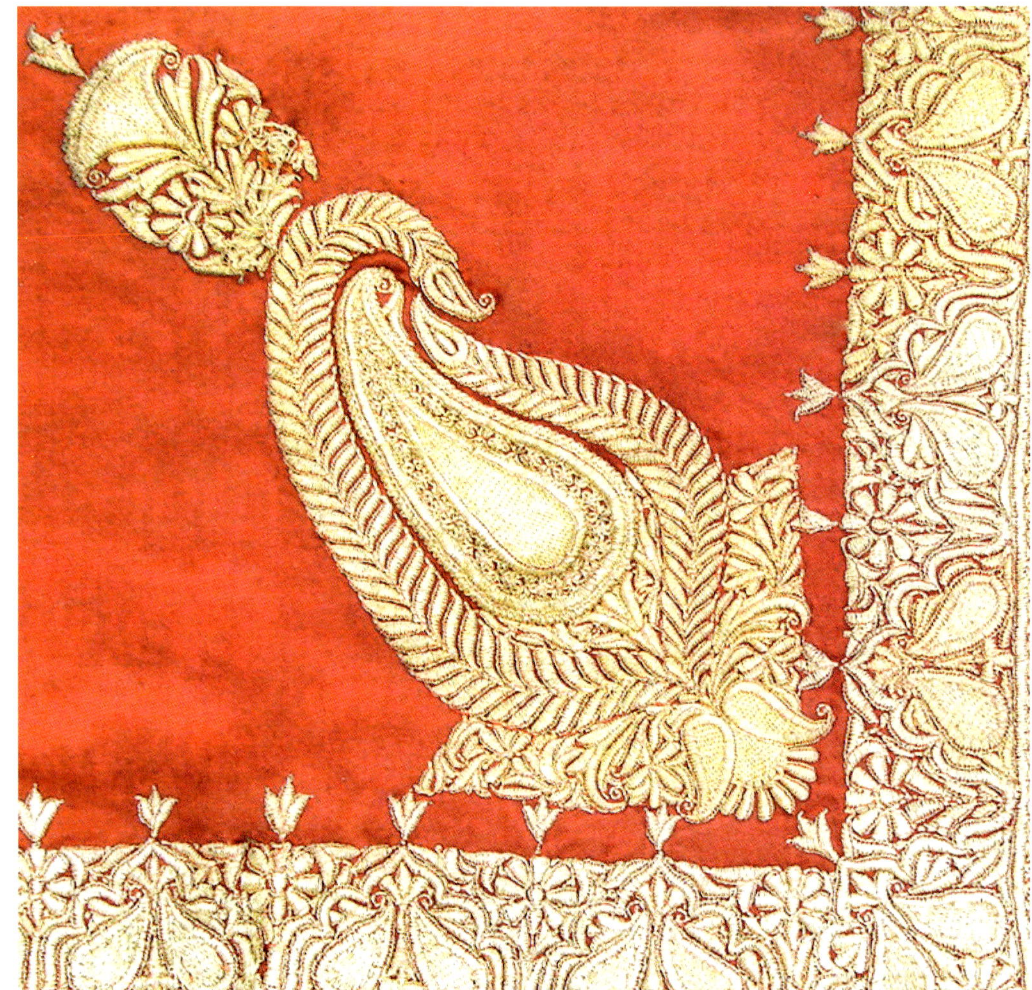

RIGHT
Pashmina woollen shawl with zari *embroidery, from twentieth century Kashmir, in the collection of Bhopal Begum family. The pashmina shawl was woven in Kashmir and embroidered at Bhopal by* zari *embroiderers. The* pallav, *border and* konia *designs are composed by the repetition of the paisley motif.*

Zardozi Embroidery

The art of original *zari* embroidery was highly encouraged during the rule of Her Highness Nawab Shah Jahan Begum in 1868. Most master craftsmen were migrants from Kanpur, Lucknow and Delhi. The technique was, in fact, introduced as one of the subjects in the curriculum prescribed for girls. *Zari* work was done using pure silver wire coated with real gold. The traditional *zardozi* work was done with the use of *salma*, *sitara* (prepared out of twisted gold thread and sequins), crinkled *badla* (delicate needle work done with silver or gold flat wires and sequins) which were used with pearls and semi-precious stones. Costumes and other garments were embroidered in a delicate and sophisticated manner, whereas the heavy embroidered work was confined to the preparation of *masnad*s (floor coverings), *kanat*s (side walls of the tents), *palan*s (elephant covers) and decorative panels. Contrasted against rich purple, maroon, bottle green and velvet, the heavy gold work appeared even richer.

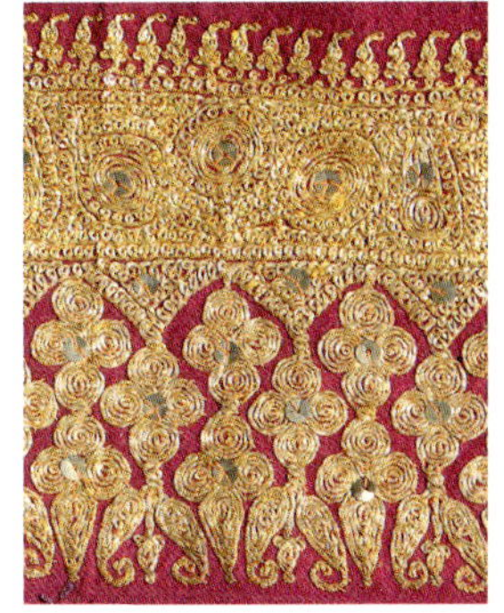

ABOVE
Detail of a zari *embroidered dupatta, from the twentieth century, in the collection of Bhopal Begum family.*

Although a number of products like saris, carpets, garments, curtains, table covers and furnishings still use the typical *zari* work, the best known item originating from Madhya Pradesh, particularly from Bhopal, continues to be the famous *batwa* (the general Hindi word used for a purse, pouch, evening bag, small leather or cloth bag with heavy *zari* work).

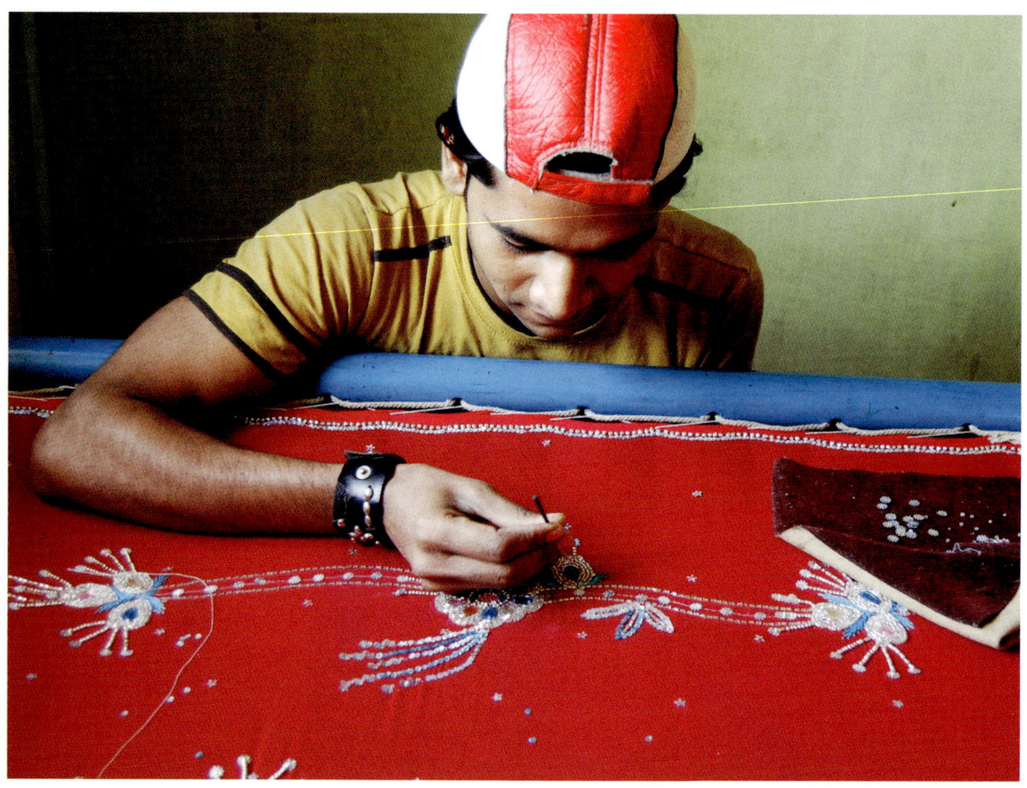

ABOVE
A craftsman intricately embroiders sequins and silver thread into silk.

The unique feature of the *batwa* is the use of traditional motifs – animals, birds, the Ashoka pillar, Sanchi Stupa, or even Buddha or Gandhi with gold patterns. Another well known item from Bhopal is a beautifully crafted, tiny box used for keeping handkerchiefs.

Folk and Tribal Paintings of Madhya Pradesh

In the Bundelkhand region comprising Gwalior, Datia, Tikamgarh, Chhatarpur, Jabalpur, Sagar, Damoh and adjoining areas, the traditional way of depicting folk related tribal paintings can be seen in the popular style known as *chitera*.

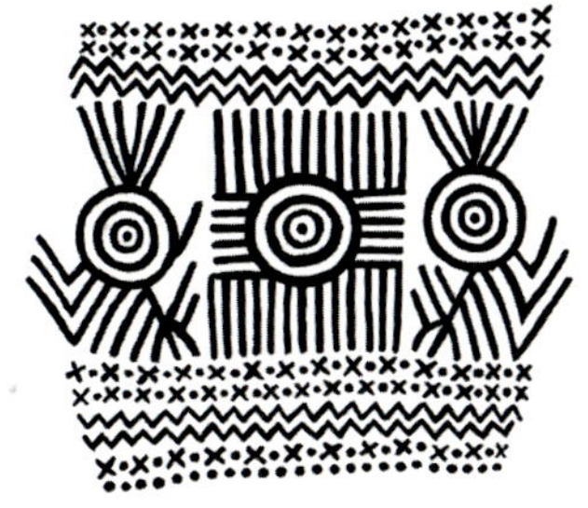

The Bhagor region comprising Jhabua, Dhar, Ratlam, Khargone and adjoining areas are inhabited by tribal groups, namely Bhils and Bhilalas. This region is especially famous for its distinct artistic tradition of painting, sculpture and basketry.

Pithora is the traditional form of wall painting signifying the advent of an auspicious occasion (like weddings, childbirth and festivals) in the family or community. With their bright colours and animated figures, *pithora* paintings reflect the joyful sentiments of their creators.

The essence of a *pithora* painting lies in its earthiness; everything from the theme to the execution has the ethnicity of rural India. The tradition of *pithora* paintings is also associated with a good harvest and fertility. The chief artist is called *lakhindra*. *Pithora* paintings comprise horses representing various tribal gods and goddesses and manifestations of Nature in various forms. The artists predominantly use cow dung plaster for walls and white lime for sketches.

ABOVE
A popular tribal tattoo design.

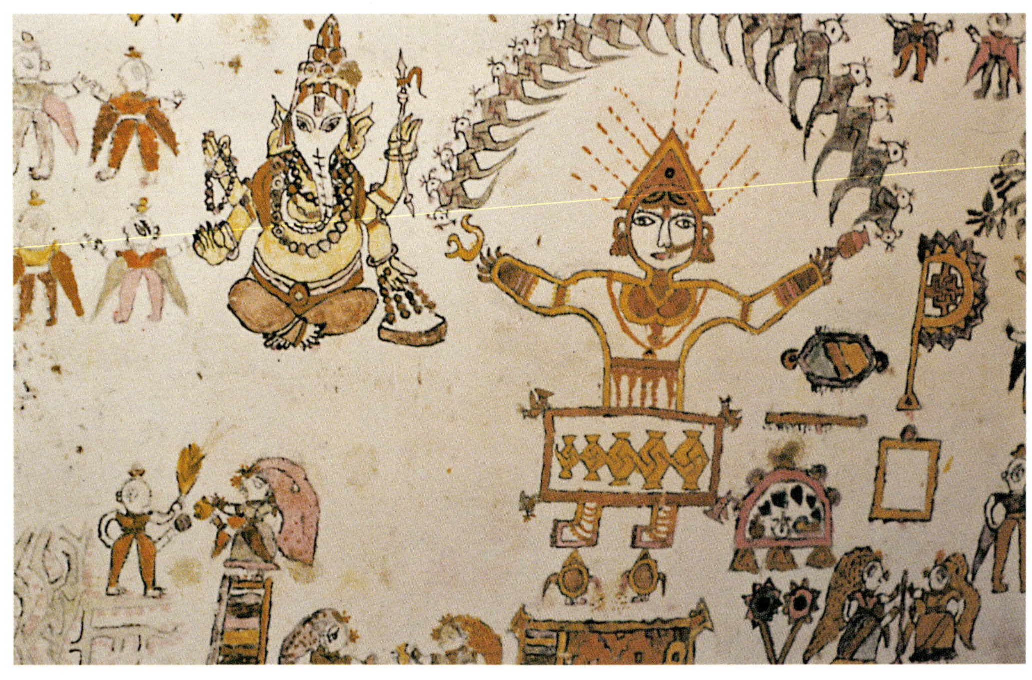

ABOVE
A wall painting made on the occasion of Diwali, depicting Ganesha and other deities.

Gondwana, comprising sub-regions of Mandla, Balaghat, Chhindwara, Seoni and Shadohl, forms the cultural hub of the region. The name Gondwana traces its origin from the long time rule of the chief tribes – Gonds, Baigas, Pardhans, Kols, Agariyas and Bharias. The art and culture of the region is heavily influenced by the Gonds and the Pardhans. The material that is used includes *geru* for the walls and doors and yellow and black clay for patterns.

RIGHT
A brightly painted wall inside a typical tribal home in Sheopur.

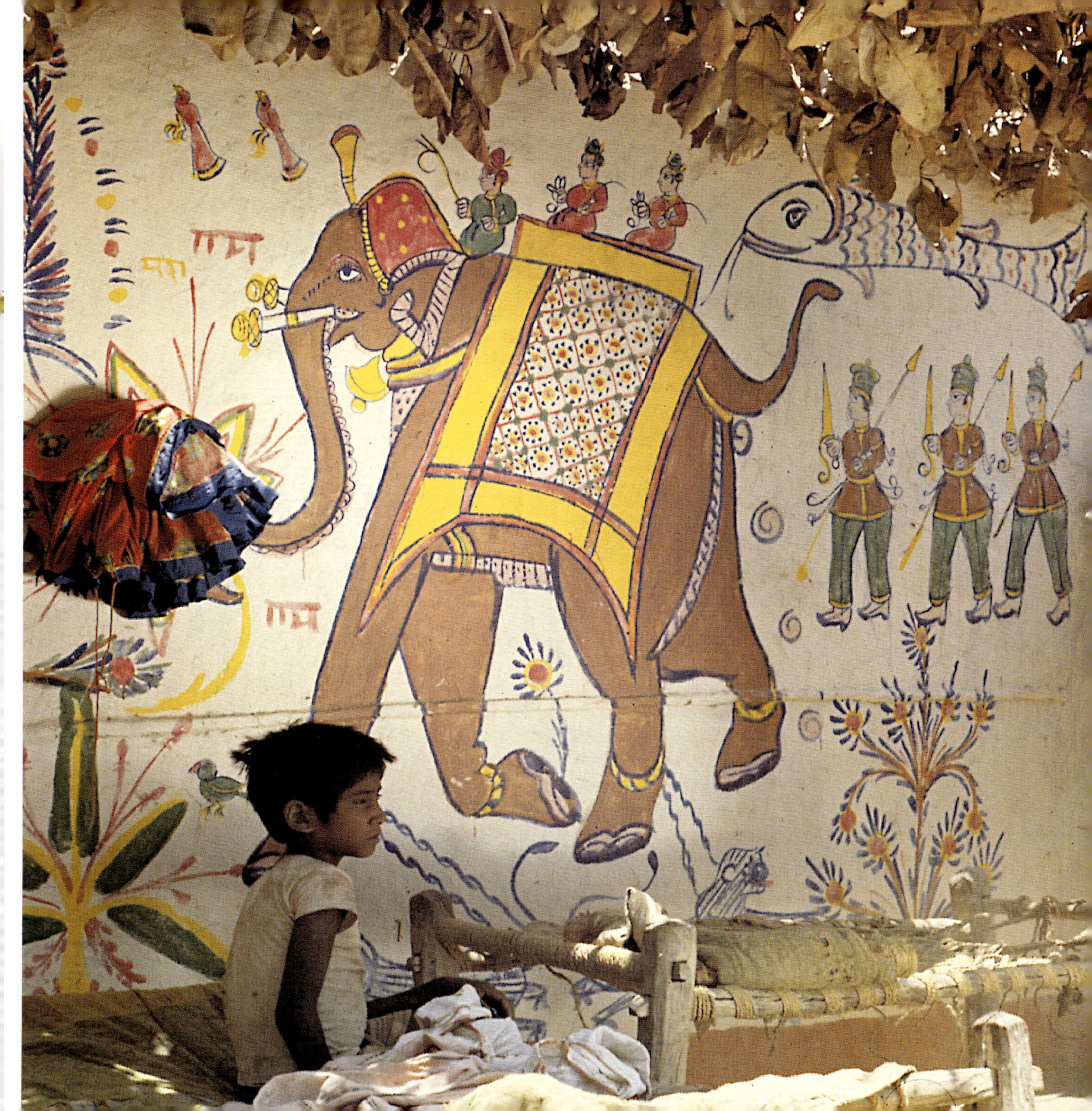

Basketry and Bamboo Products

Madhya Pradesh has dense vegetation cover and huge forest areas. Bamboo is one of the richest natural resources, particularly in the tribal districts of the state. Balaghat, Betul, Seoni, Guna, Alirajpur and Mandla happen to be some of the bamboo intensive areas where, due to easy access to bamboo, basket weaving and bamboo products have become an important craft in the region and in the state.

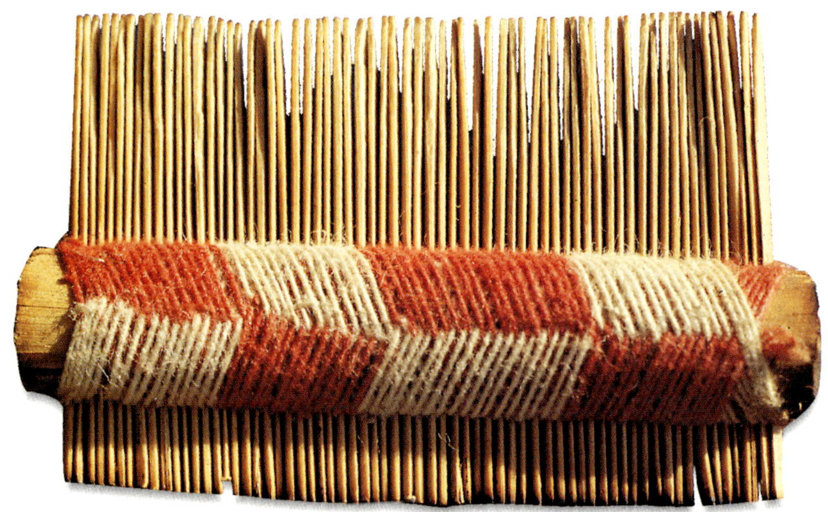

RIGHT
A bamboo comb, typically used by Gond and Baiga tribals in Mandla.

RIGHT
Basket weavers at work, crafting bamboo baskets in Mandla.

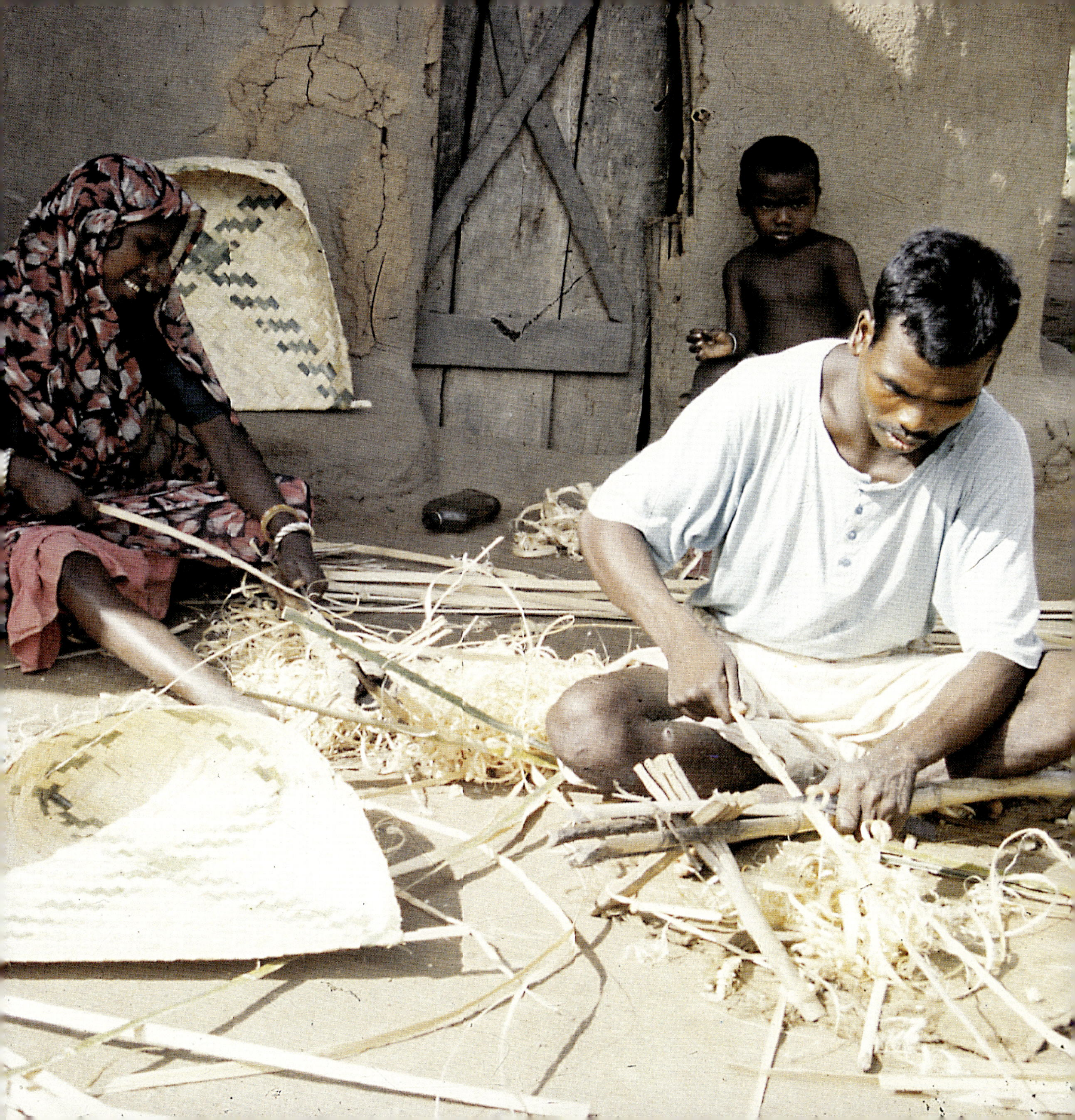

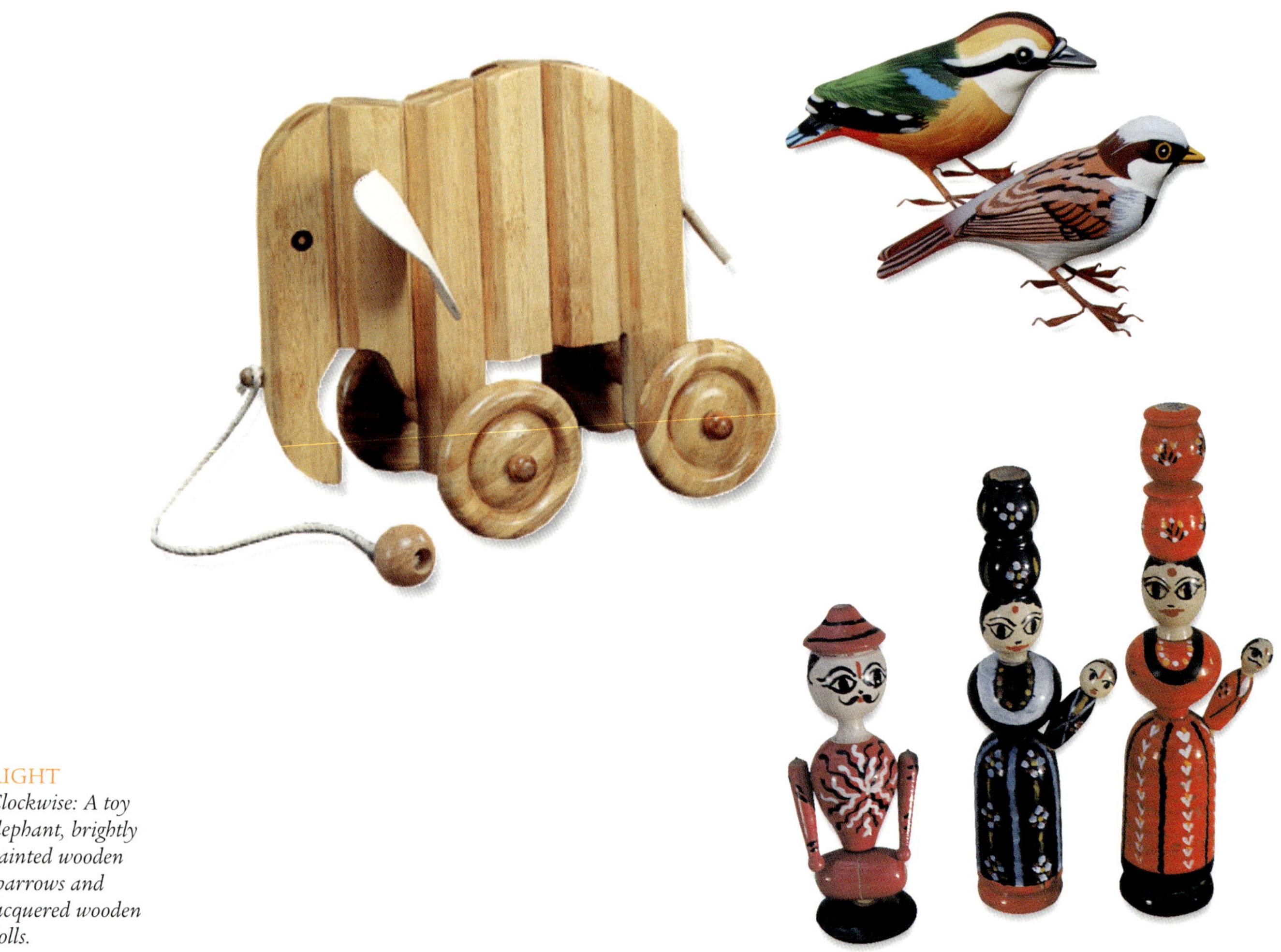

RIGHT
Clockwise: A toy elephant, brightly painted wooden sparrows and lacquered wooden dolls.

Dolls and Toys

Madhya Pradesh is well known for its lacquered wooden dolls and lamp stands, particularly the areas of Sheopur, Hoshangabad, Itarsi, Budhni (Sehore district) and Rewa. Papier mâché products are prevalent in Ujjain, while Indore is famous for leather toys. Gwalior has a distinctive style of toys named after a master craftsperson, Battobai, which is created out of rugs and paper. In Jhabua, in the predominantly tribal belt, toy making has been encouraged by the Khadi Board.

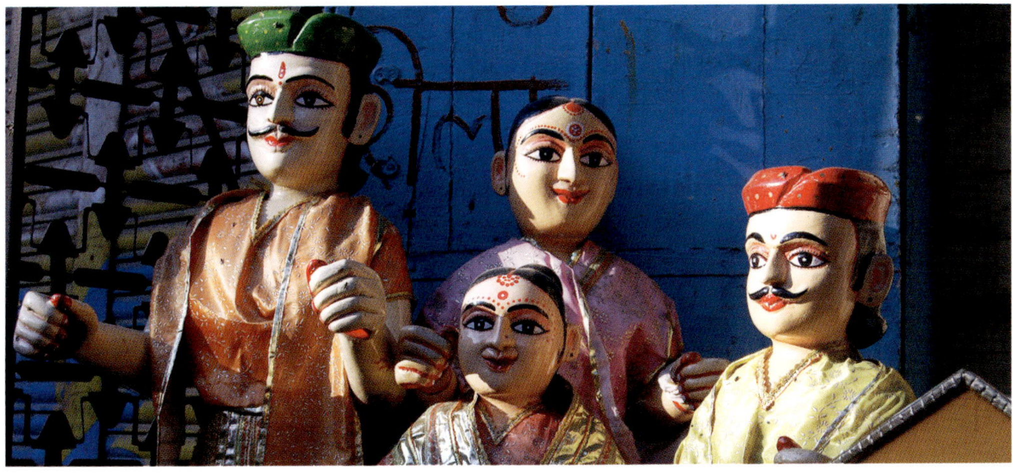

LEFT
Painted wooden Gangaur dolls, Ujjain.

Metal Craft

Mandsaur district is famous for its fine craft of gold, popularly known as *thewa* work. While Shivpuri's craftspeople make ornamental boxes, Karera is known for its iron work including traditional locks and nutcrackers. In Khajuraho, there are abundant indications of sales of typical tribal arts, crafts and utensils. Tikamgarh is well known for its brass products like chariots, brass horses with wheels and nutcrackers. A number of craftspeople are still working on casting for ornaments made in brass, bronze, white metal and silver. Lateri in Vidisha district is also famous for nutcrackers and razors.

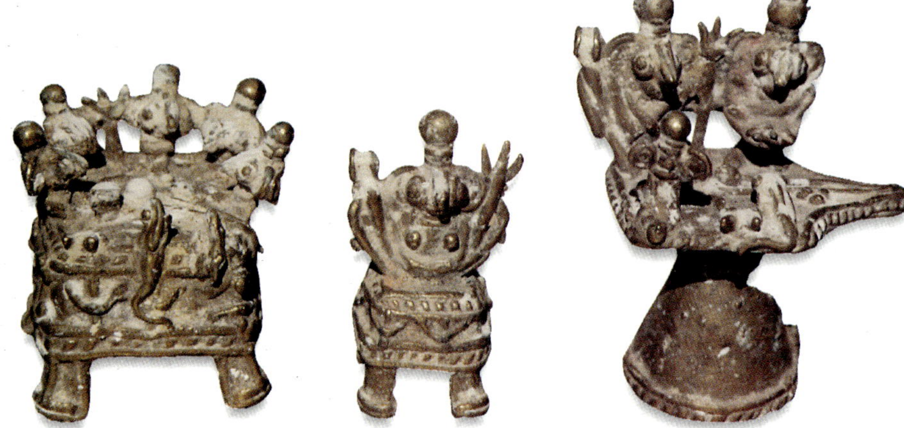

RIGHT
Traditional metal idols of the Gond deity, Mahadev from Hoshangabad. These antique idols are more than 200 years old.

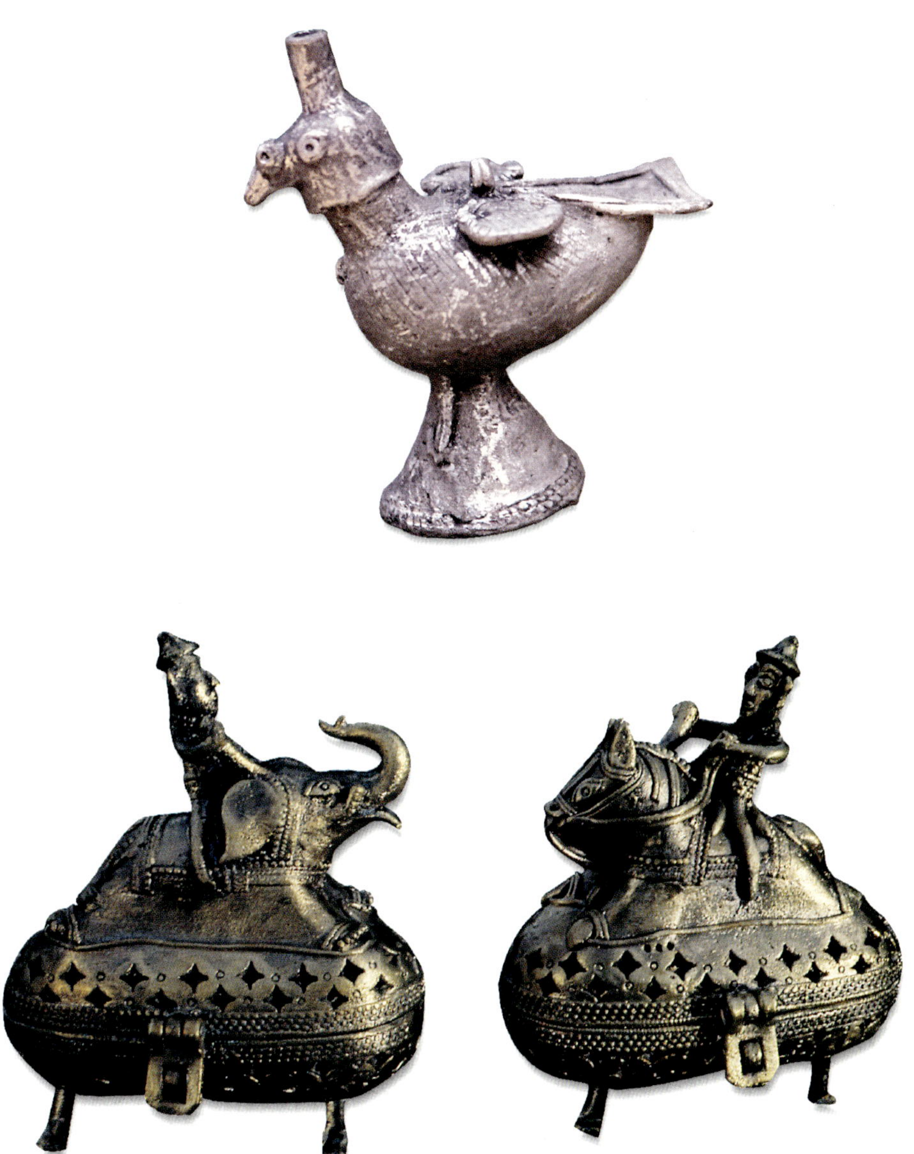

ABOVE AND LEFT
A metal lamp in the shape of a bird from Betul; ornamental boxes from Tikamgarh.

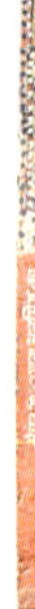

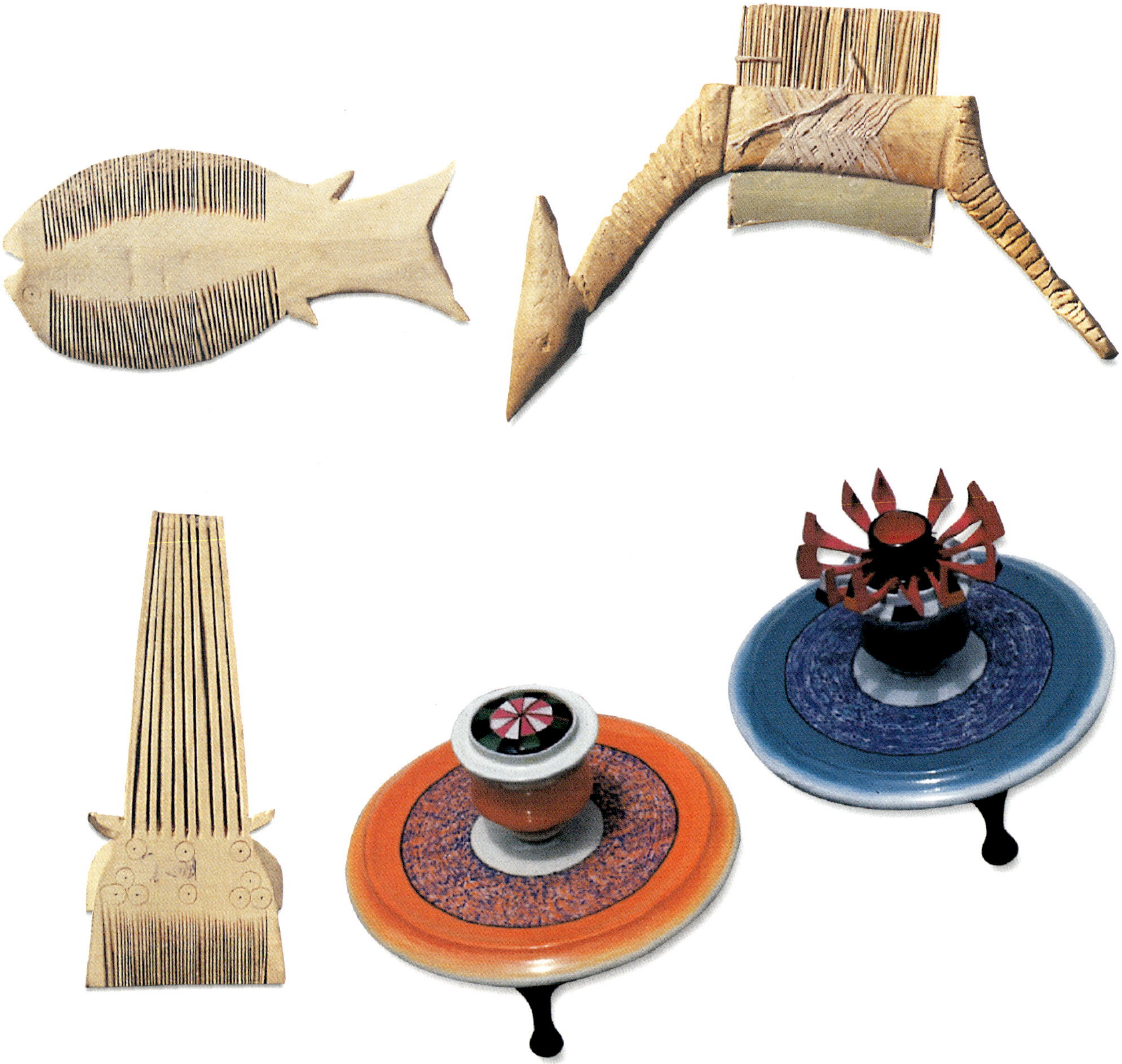

RIGHT
Wood and bamboo tribal craft from Mandla; itradan *used to store perfume oil from Sheopur.*

Wood Craft

The artistic skill of the tribal people of Madhya Pradesh is visible in their own homes, where they use intricately carved poles, door panels, ceilings, frames and other such forms. The Baiga and Agaria tribal community members make special doors using two panels, each made out of a single plank and decorated with motifs of animals, birds, human figures, floral and geometric patterns. The Agarias are known to first make planks followed by relief work of a relatively high degree of skill.

There is another form which is very popular and that is the memorial pillars of Hoshangabad, Betul, Pachmarhi and Nimar villages inhabited by the Korku tribe. These pillars are made out of teak wood.

The other common forms of wood craft include bird figures configured in the dance form. Although wood carvers use very simple technique and tools which are made of iron, the results are often surprisingly detailed and delicate.

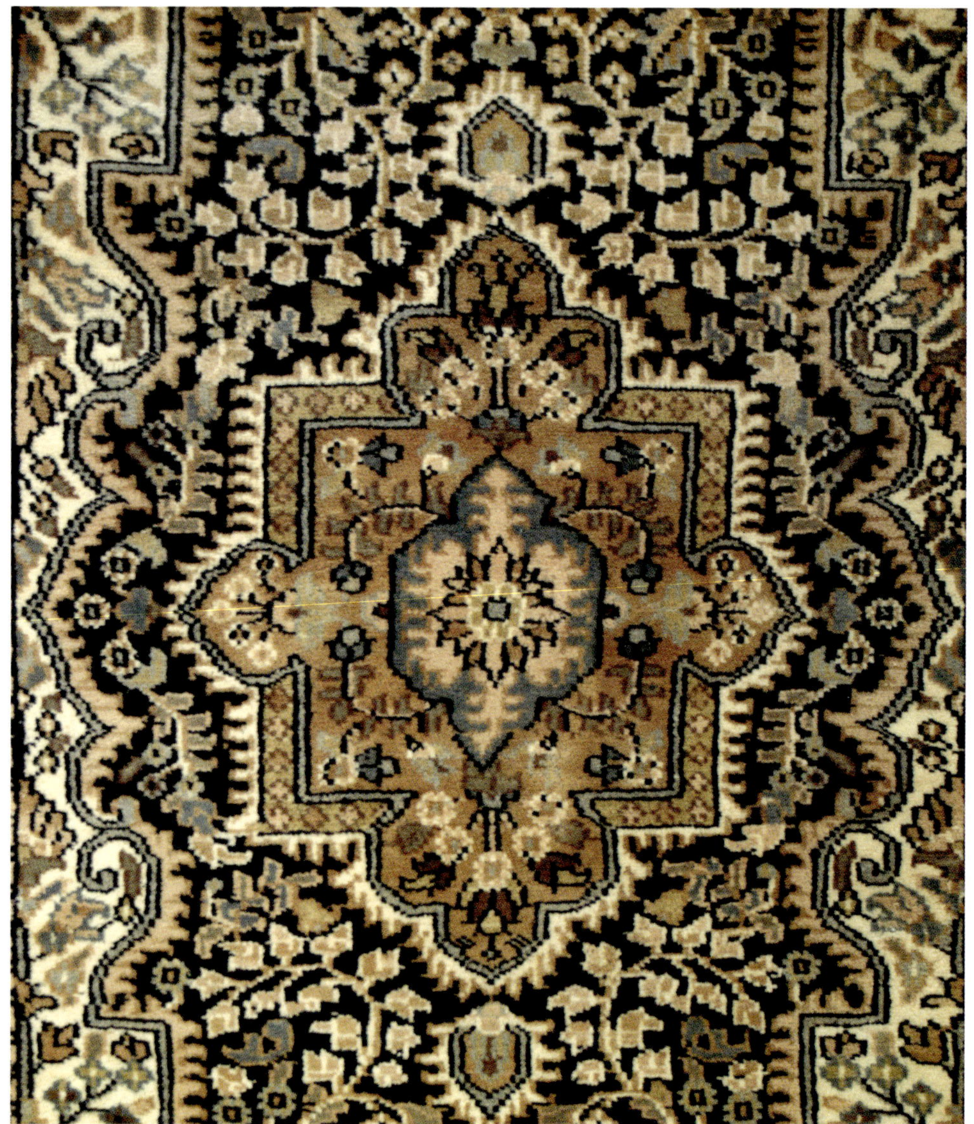

RIGHT
Detail of a Gwalior silk carpet with a fusion of typical geometric and traditional motifs.

Carpets and Durries

The districts of Shahdol, Rewa and Sidhi adjoining the districts of Uttar Pradesh (particularly Bhadoi, Mirzapur and Shahjahanpur) have a long history of carpet making and durrie weaving dating back to the fourteenth and seventeenth century AD. This is largely due to the fact that the region has witnessed a continuous chain of migration of the descendants of craftsmen. In this context, the case of the craftsmen of Gwalior is peculiar. They are descendants of the craftsmen of Agra. Even after their migration to Gwalior, they received (and continue to receive) support from the carpet exporters of Agra. Today, Gwalior is recognised as one of the most important manufacturing centres of carpet weaving in Central India. Besides woollen and silk carpets, the weavers of this area also weave carpets in artificial silk. Other interesting aspects of carpet weaving in Gwalior include use of natural colours for dyeing apart from synthetic dyes and the exceptional use of floral motifs.

PAGE 52
The opulent interior of the Lalbagh Palace, Indore.

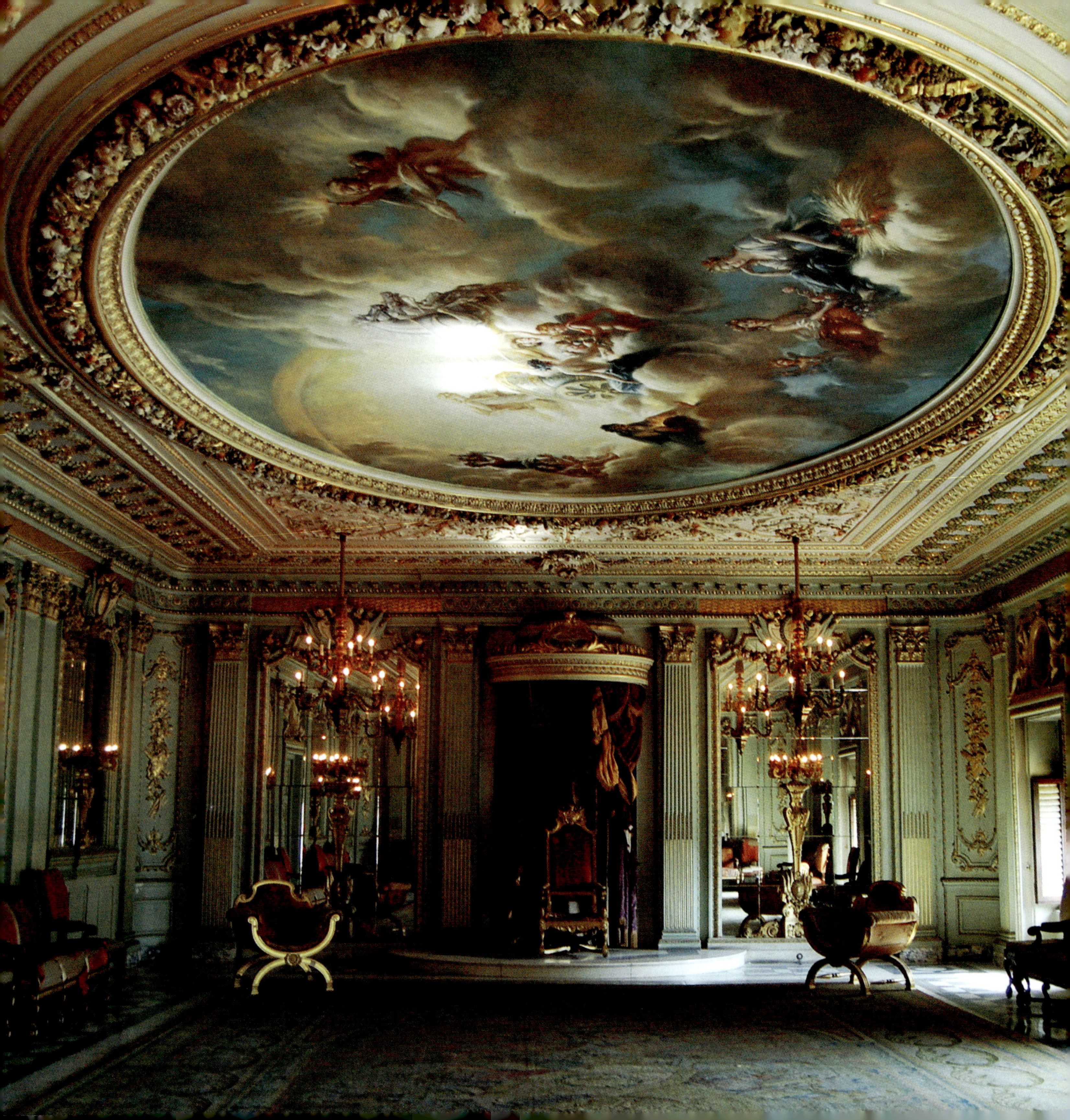

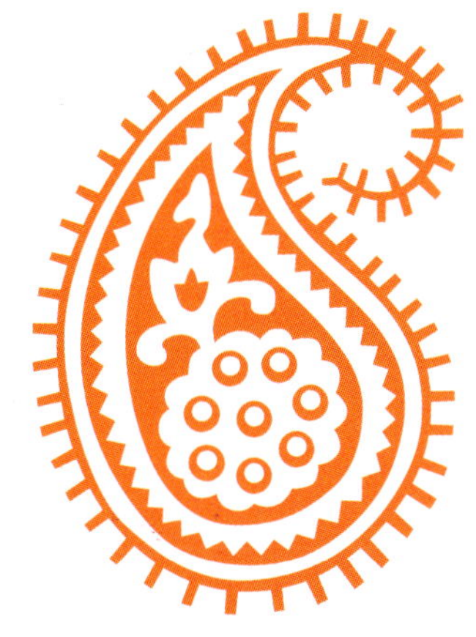

The Royal Heritage of Madhya Pradesh

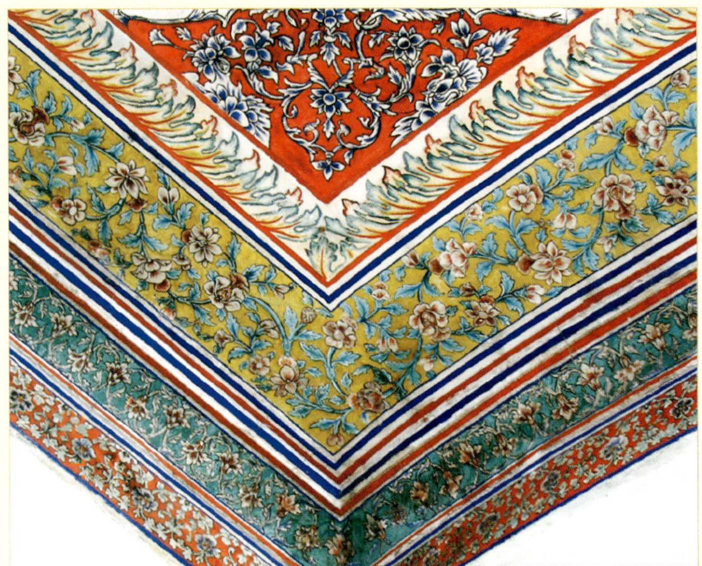

LEFT
A detail of a corner ceiling painting in mineral and natural colours, in Moti Mahal, Gwalior. The palace was built during the reign of Jayaji Rao Scindia in the late nineteenth century.

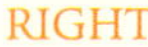

RIGHT
An ornate brass chandelier at Lalbagh Palace, Indore.

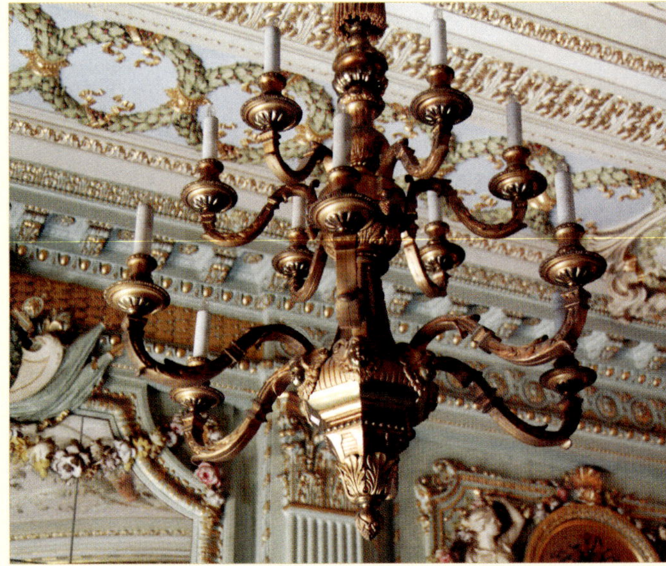

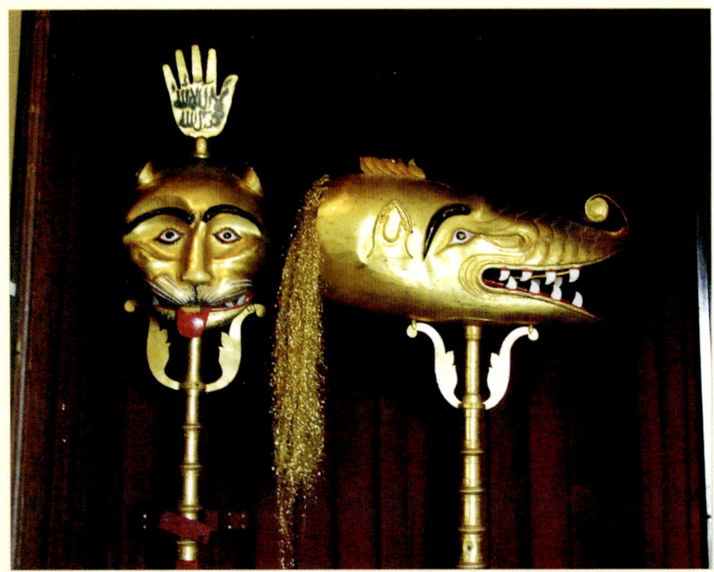

LEFT
Alam, *brass metal emblems from the late nineteenth century, presently in the collection of Jai Vilas Palace Museum, Gwalior.*

Between the fifteenth and the nineteenth century, in Central India, now Madhya Pradesh, the Scindias of Gwalior and the Holkars of Indore were great patrons of the arts. Malhar Rao Holkar (1694 - 1766) established the family's rule over Indore. He was succeeded by his daughter-in-law, Rani Ahilyabai Holkar, who reigned between 1767 - 1795. Rani Ahilyabai, as she was affectionately called, was an exemplary ruler. She moved the capital to Maheshwar, south of Indore on the Narmada River. Rani Ahilyabai was a great builder and patron of many Hindu temples, which embellished Maheshwar and Indore. Furthermore, Rani Ahilyabai single-handedly revived the Maheshwar sari industry, re-locating weavers from Surat to weave saris and turban cloth for royalty.

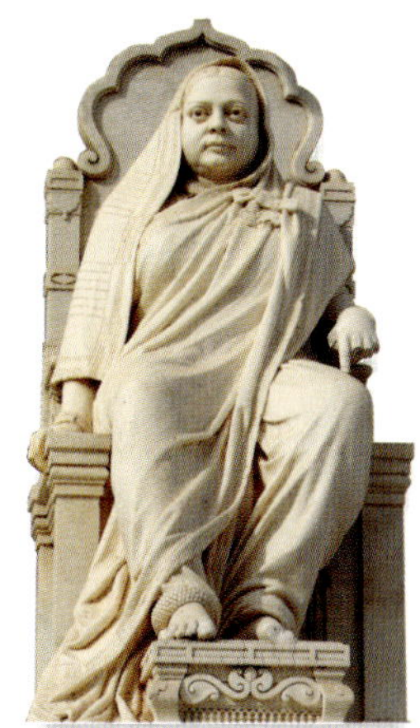

In the beginning of the nineteenth century, with the firm establishment of the East India Company in India, the Scindias and Holkars came under the influence of European culture — the young princes were sent off to Europe for further studies, where they were exposed to an entirely different aesthetic of art and culture. This influence is evident in the architecture, wall paintings, furniture, and products they imported or got specially made for their palaces.

The famous Jai Vilas Palace of Gwalior and Lalbagh Palace of Indore are the peculiar examples of an Indo-European style which developed in that period and deserve to be examined in some detail.

ABOVE
Marble statue of Amma Maharaj in Gwalior, part of the Amma Maharaj Chhatri *at Phool Bagh.*

A few kilometres south of the Gwalior Fort, the city of Lashkar was established in 1809. By 1829, Lashkar was already a full-fledged town with

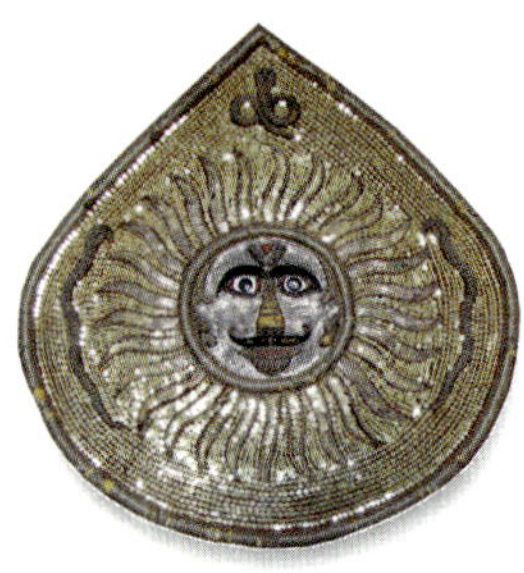

ABOVE
A detail of a zari *embroidered emblem of the Scindia rulers, from the early twentieth century at Gwalior, presently in the collection of Jai Vilas Palace Museum.*

RIGHT
Gold and mirror work dating from the nineteenth century on the ceiling of the Darbar Hall, Moti Mahal, Gwalior.

wide streets, stone houses and a proper sewage system. It seemed to be the perfect place to build a dazzling architectural masterpiece. The gleaming white Jai Vilas Palace, built by Lt Col Sir Michael Filose, was designed to resemble an Italian palazzo. It was built between 1872 and 74, to welcome the Prince of Wales on his visit to the city. Although the palace was executed in sandstone, it was painted a brilliant white to simulate marble.

Though the present Maharaja of Gwalior still lives in the palace, thirty-five of its rooms house the Scindia Museum, which displays royal memorabilia. The museum boasts of a remarkable collection of artefacts, culled from all over the world. A crystal staircase winds its way up to the spectacular Durbar Hall. The arched ceiling, with exquisite gold leaf work, carries two of the world's largest and most magnificent chandeliers, each weighing over three tons and holding 248 candles. The chandeliers were gilded with fifty-six kilograms of gold. Spread out across this very hall is the largest carpet in Asia, which took twelve years to weave. The rooms of Jai Vilas Palace and Scindia Museum are filled with other curiosities like a Rolls Royce on rails, stuffed tigers and a life size statue of Leda. There is also a silver train with cut glass wagons which served guests as it chugged around on miniature rails on the table and swords that were once worn by Mughal emperors Aurangazeb and Shah Jahan. A German bubble car, the jewelled slippers that belonged to Chinkoo Rani and hunting trophies and portraits can also be found here.

Besides colonial furniture, a large variety of carved wooden furniture can be seen at Jai Vilas Palace. Densely carved Malabar woodwork in black

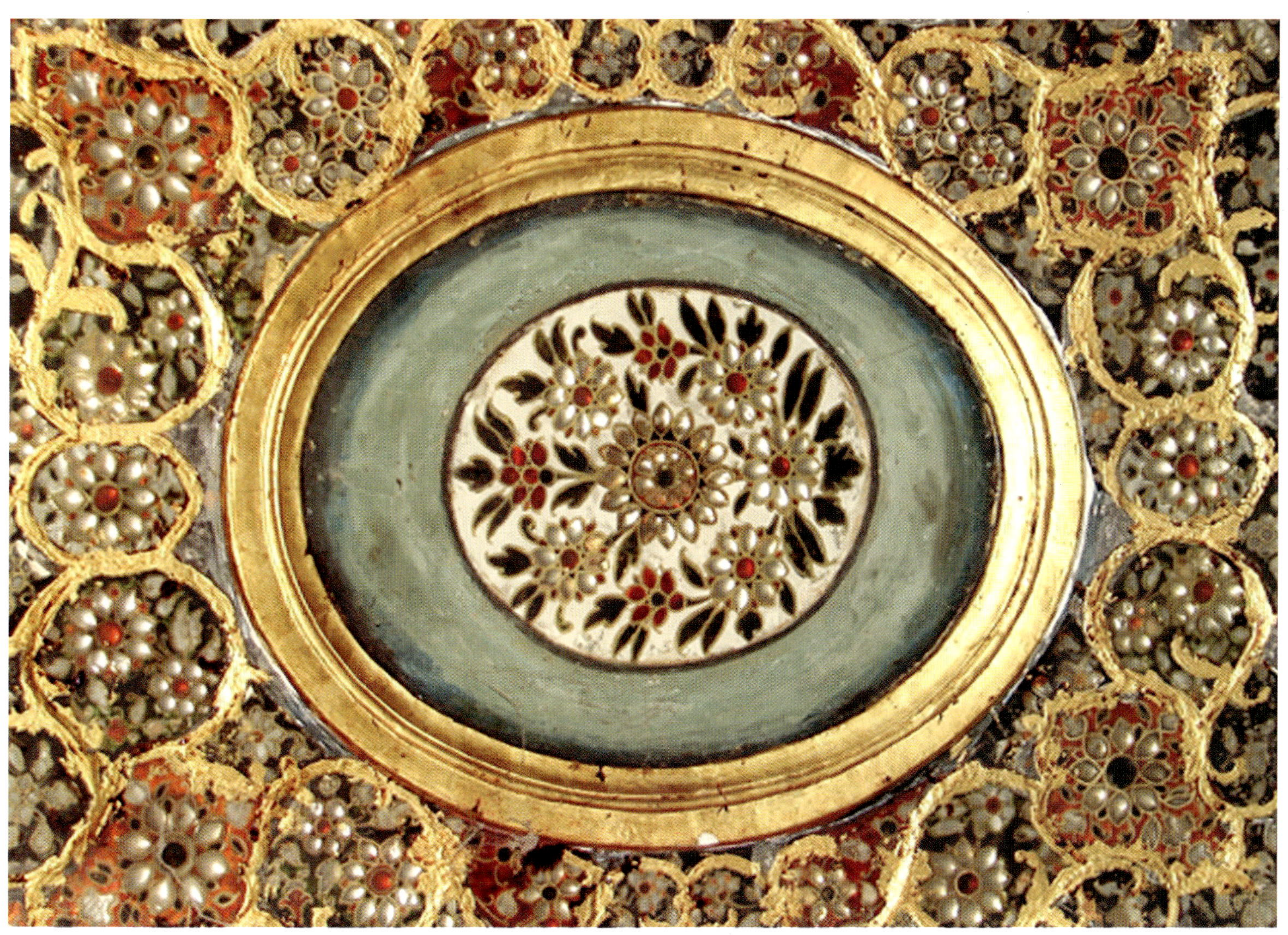

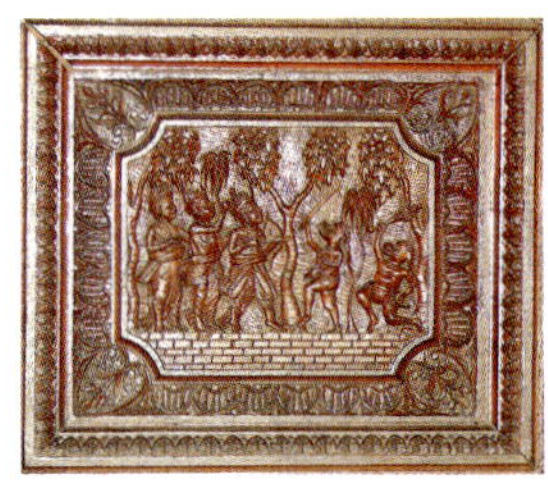

ebony wood, delicately carved walnut wood work of Kashmir, heavily carved beds showing figures in the Maratha style of clothing, swings, palanquins and elephant seats, all of exceptionally fine quality, depict the high level of craftsmanship of that time.

Lalbagh Palace, built during the rule of Holkars, is a beautiful example of the splendour and lifestyle of the Holkar dynasty. It was designed by Triggs & Co. of Calcutta. Spread over an area of twenty-eight hectares, Lalbagh Palace is a brilliant blend of traditional motifs and modern conveniences.

Its construction began in 1886 under Tukoji Rao Holkar II, and was carried out in three phases, the final phase completed in 1921 under Tukoji Rao Holkar III. Till recently, the descendants of the Holkars lived in this palace, a part of which has been converted into a museum, which displays rare paintings and other objects from the golden era of Holkar rule.

ABOVE
Section of a bed, Jai Vilas Palace, Gwalior.

Cast in iron and brought from England, the entrance gates of the palace are reminiscent of those found in Buckingham Palace, London. The billiard room is noted for its jewel-encrusted portraits of Tukoji Rao, who completed the palace. A spring-mounted floor in the ballroom, marble columns, chandeliers, stained-glass windows and stuffed tigers add to the opulence of the palace.

RIGHT
Main hall showing gold work of the late nineteenth century at Moti Mahal, Gwalior.

The restored rooms within the palace now function as a museum. It exhibits a variety of furniture and their ornamentation in the late Regency

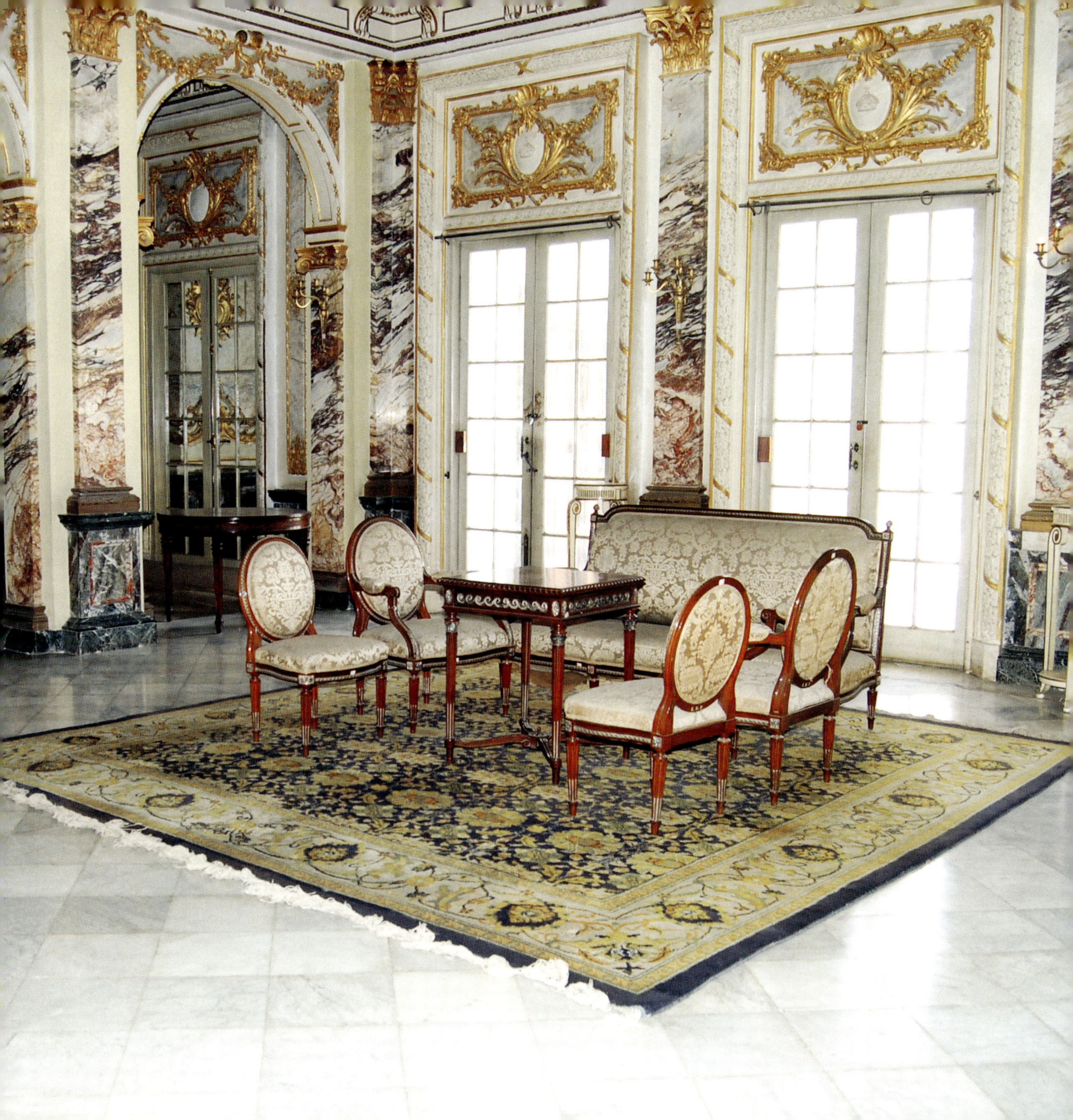

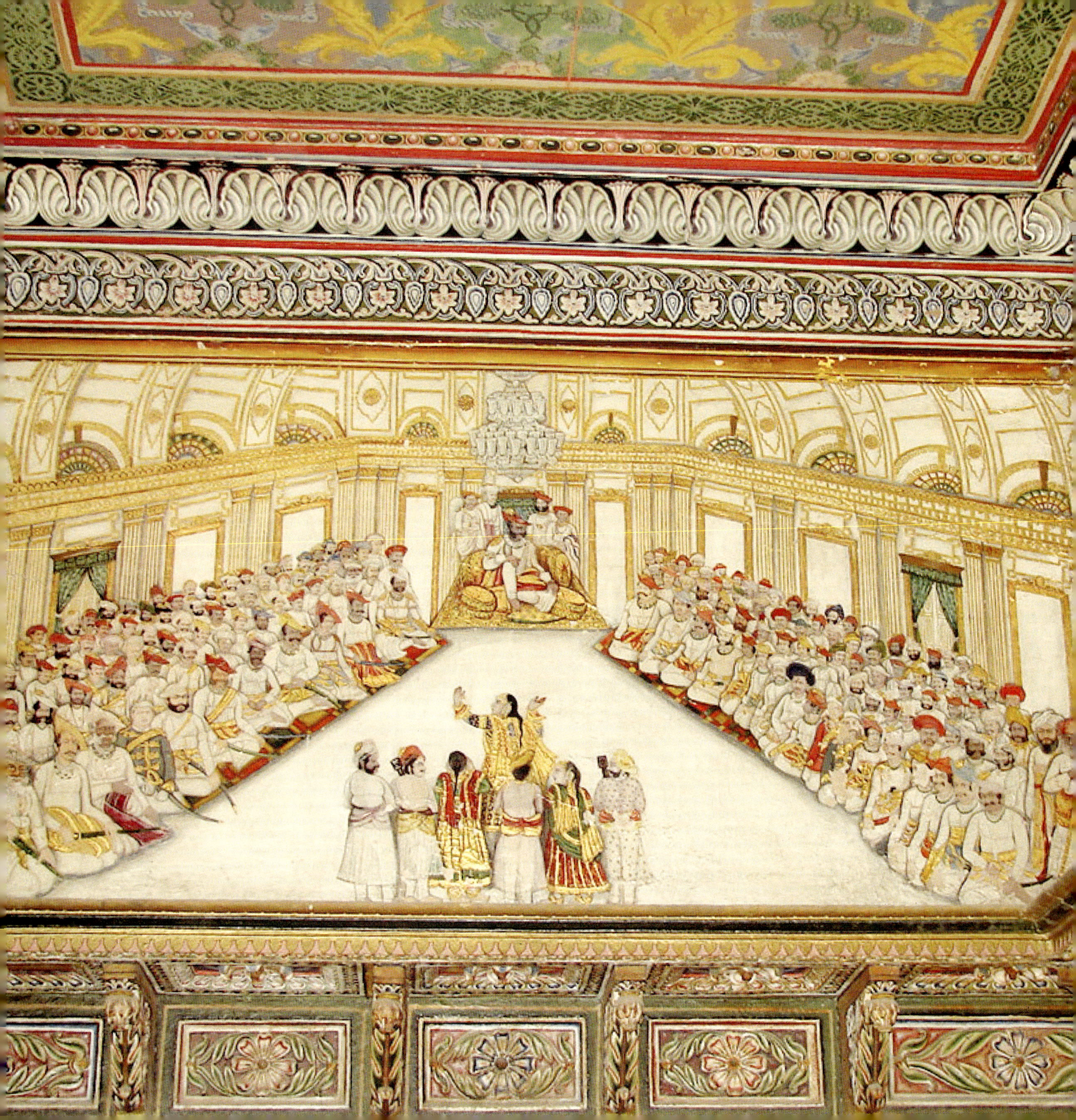

and early Gregorian styles. There are two attractive rooms, which display the articles of the Mughal era. The coin collection on the first floor dates back to the early Muslim period. Among the unique displays are Italian sculptures and intricately inlaid boxes. Other exhibits include prehistoric artefacts, miniatures and contemporary Indian paintings. A reflection of their taste, grandeur and life style, it is a blend of the decorative and Renaissance styles, and in its day, was one of the most elegant residences in India. It is being developed by the Government of Madhya Pradesh as a cultural centre. The main attractions are the splendidly proportioned and furnished rooms, with frescoed ceilings and gilded ornamental mouldings. The architecture and decoration of this palace, inhabited by the Holkars till 1978, reflect the highly westernised aesthetic sensibility of the later Holkars. Tukoji Rao III was the last incumbent of this magnificent palace. It is unclear as to whether the artisans who had created the furniture, wall paintings, panels, mirror and picture frames, tapestries and furnishings, durries and floor spreads and other decorative items were Indians, or whether these objects were created by a group of local artisans under the supervision of European artists. A new type of relief work on walls, pillars and ceilings was introduced which was created with the help of a new material called plaster of Paris. Italian fresco paintings were introduced to decorate ceilings and walls of the palaces.

LEFT
A wall painting from the late nineteenth century depicting the darbar *of a Scindia ruler, painted in natural and mineral colours, at Moti Mahal, Gwalior.*

During the peak of the Scindia and Holkar dynasties, various crafts of the region flourished. Crafts, such as carpet weaving, glazed pottery, hand painted playing cards, cast iron items, hand block printed textile, Chanderi and Maheshwari sari weaving, lacquered wood work dolls and

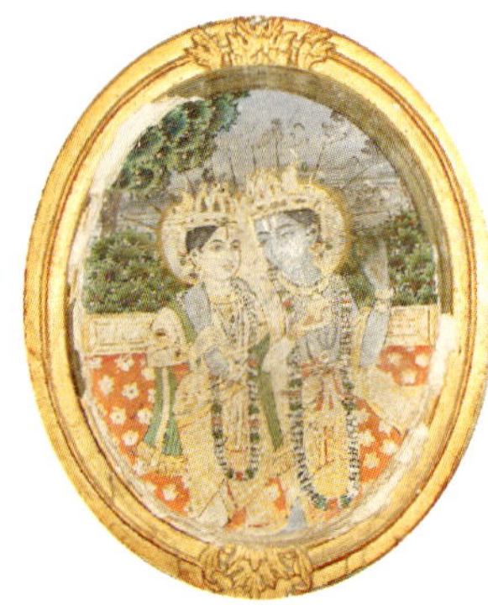

toys, *zardozi* embroidery, sheet metal work and metal utensil making, were all given royal patronage. Stone craftsmanship has always excelled in Madhya Pradesh, as is evident from the exquisite stone carvings of temples in Khajuraho. The stone craft of Gwalior in particular became famous under the royal patronage of the Scindia kings. Furthermore, the carving skills of the artisans were recognised by the English officers. Products like carved stone furniture, garden furniture, fountains, pillars, brackets, grills and pots were made to suit European tastes.

Musuems in Madhya Pradesh also provide clues about the state's rich heritage, royal and otherwise. It is evident from several museums across the state that arts and crafts played a prominent role in the creative output of society as early as the first century BC. The Gwalior Archaeological Museum houses a large and varied collection of antiquities, collected from Gwalior and its adjoining areas. The sculptural wealth in particular reflects the development of sculptural art and style in India from first century BC to the seventeenth century AD with the sculptures from Mitawali being from the earliest collection of the museum. The colossal figures, belonging to the Kushana period (second century BC to third century AD), shown in heavy garments and ornaments, indicate the kind of attire and accessories worn at the time.

ABOVE
A glass painting depicting Radha and Krishna, part of a pillar decoration, painted with oil colours during the late nineteenth century, at Moti Mahal, Gwalior.

The State Museum in Bhopal is also home to numerous sculptures, epigraphs, manuscripts, textiles, weapons and Bagh Miniature paintings. The textile display in particular showcases the exquisite embroidery patronised by the Nawabs of Bhopal, and includes traditional costumes and headgear. The Royal Gallery houses a collection of fine metal, ceramic and wood crafts; toys, jewellery, vases and boxes are only some of the pieces on display.

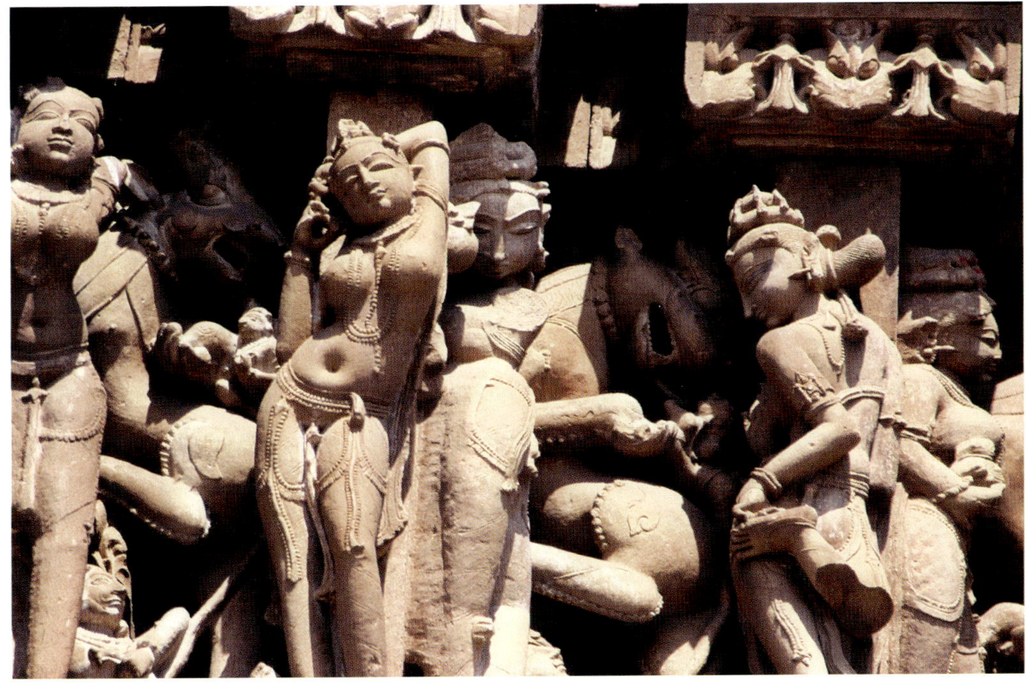

LEFT
Detail of stone carvings at a temple in Khajuraho.

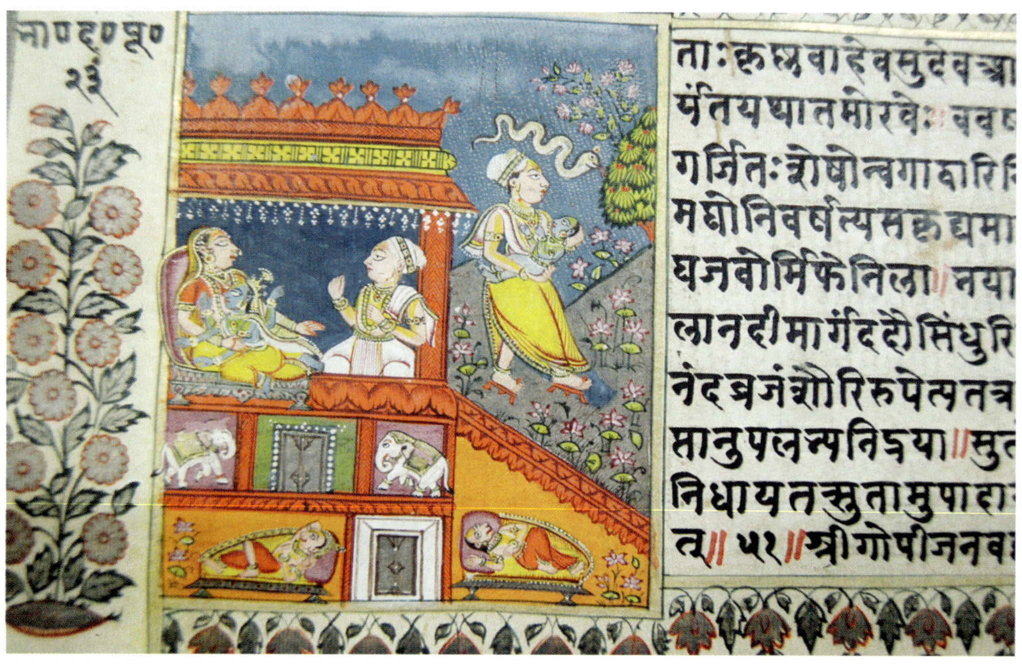

LEFT AND ABOVE RIGHT
Illustrations of hand written pothees, *dating from the early twentieth century, painted by local painters of Gwalior and Ujjain. They are painted with natural and earth colours, and are presently in the collection of the Scindia Museum of Vukram University, Ujjain.*

In Ujjain, the craft of making hand written and painted *pothee*s (scrolls) reached its height under royal patronage. This craft was also popular in Gwalior and Indore. These *pothee*s were written and painted for royal families. A very good collection of these *pothee*s can be seen at the Manuscript Museum in Ujjain. The *chiteras*, or folk painters have painted many wall murals in *haveli*s, temples, *chhatri*s (cenotaphs) and courts under royal patronage. Moti Mahal in Gwalior still has some of the excellent examples of these paintings on its walls, ceilings and doors.

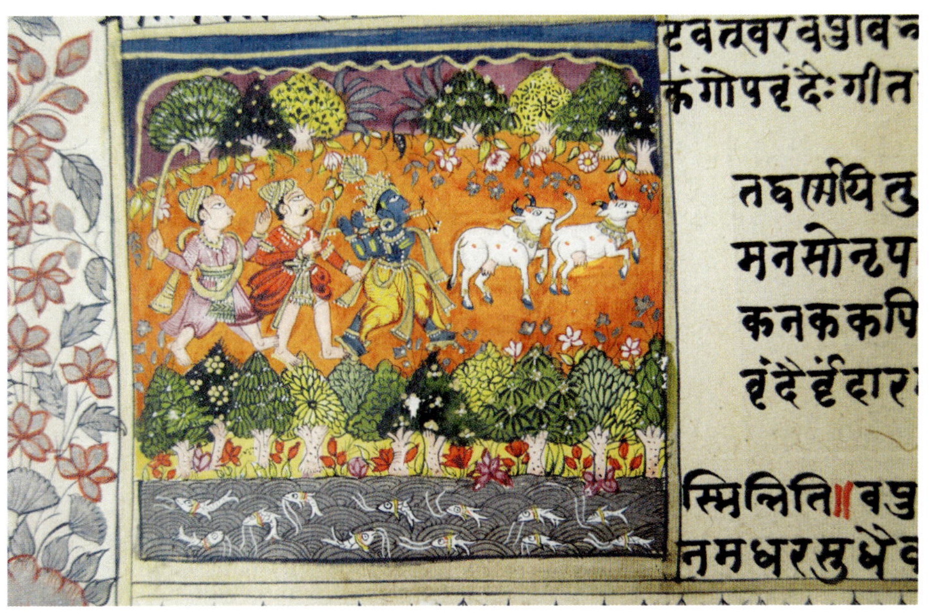

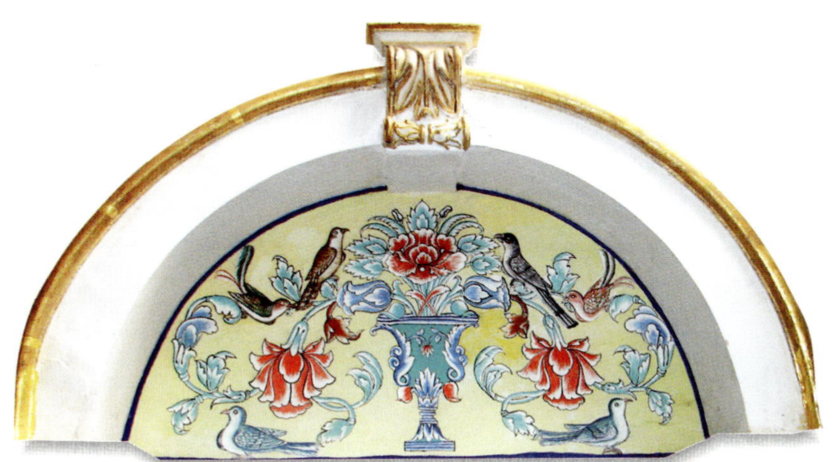

RIGHT
A detail of a ceiling painting with gold work, painted with natural colours, from the nineteenth century at Moti Mahal, Gwalior.

PAGE 66
A local artisan at work making a wooden chest with traditional artwork.

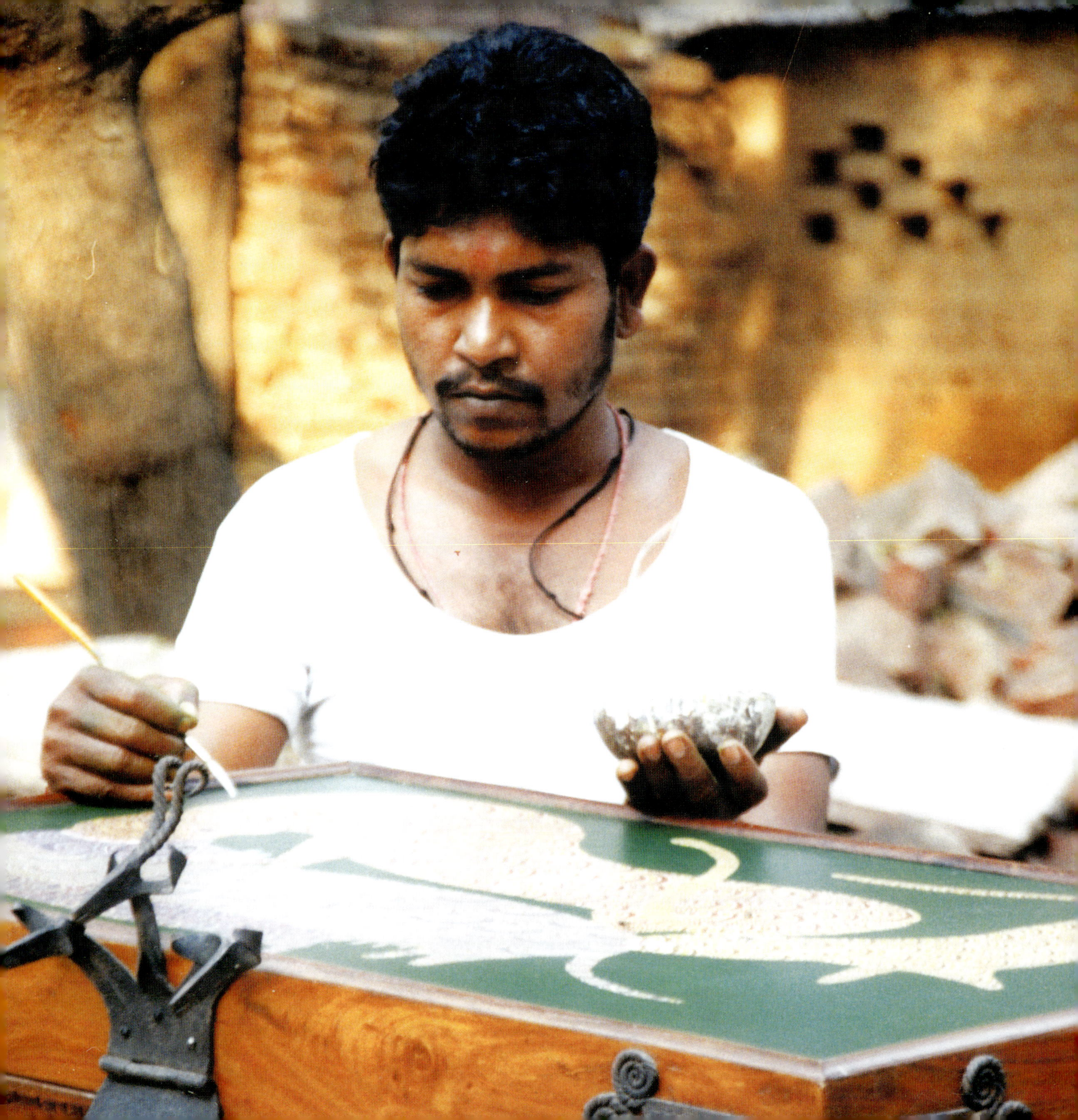

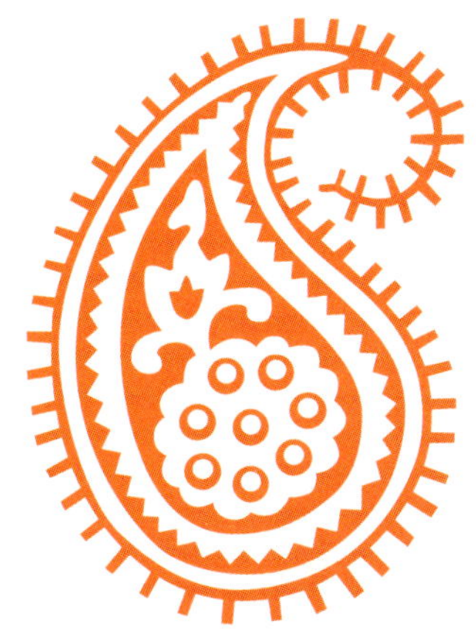

Contemporary Expressions of Living Heritage

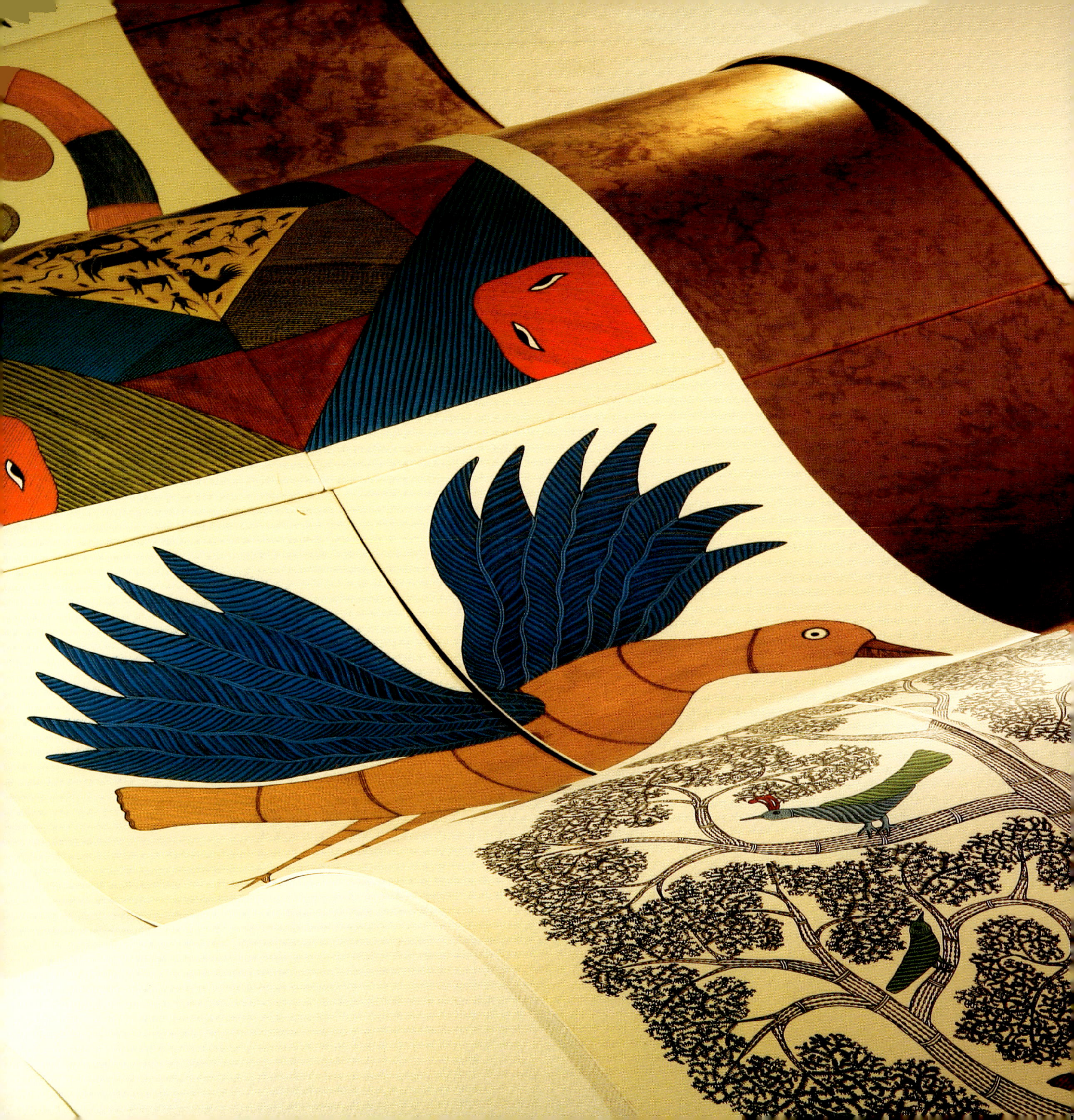

Arts and Crafts as Cultural Industries

In a global context, the Indian handicraft, handloom, khadi and village industries sector is best understood as an integral part of a creative industrial expression, uniquely positioned as a continuum of rich heritage and tradition, known in its contemporary context as living heritage and culture.

The arts and crafts of any state falls under the purview of cultural industries. According to the UNESCO framework, cultural industries are those industries which produce tangible or intangible artistic and creative outputs which also have a potential for income generation using cultural assets and production of knowledge based goods and services, both traditional and contemporary. In essence, cultural industries use creativity as well as cultural and intellectual knowledge to produce products and services with social and cultural meaning.

LEFT
The Ashoka Hotel lobby ceiling in New Delhi, decorated with the artwork of Bhajju Shyam, a Gond tribal artist.

Following the UNESCO charter, the importance of culture and creative potential is being increasingly recognised by the world over as the primary impetus of this traditional knowledge-based sector of economy and is the key to more sustainable development models. India is strategically positioned, having a large variety of living, skill-based traditions, and a highly versatile creative population to add value to the rich heritage of

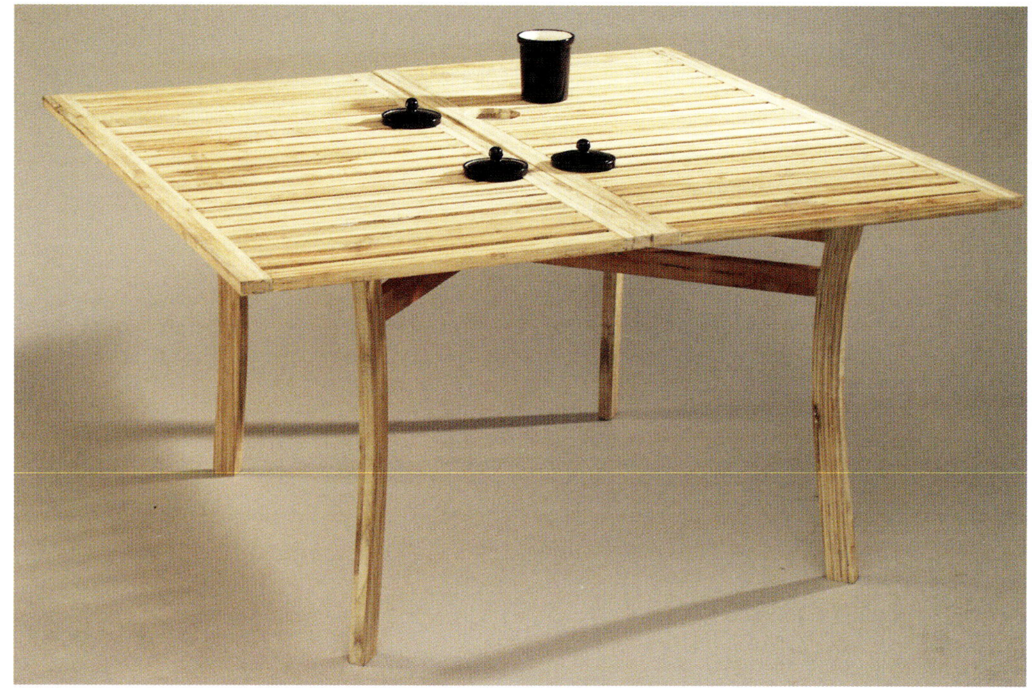

traditional products, thereby creating a demand for these products in the global market. The creative industrial sector is one of the most dynamic sectors of both global trade and the domestic market, with a high requirement of manpower, high value-added content and strong employment linkages, especially in the informal sector of the economy for small and medium-size enterprises.

ABOVE
A trendy table made with bamboo.

New Policy Initiatives in Madhya Pradesh

The Madhya Pradesh government has been an active facilitator in promoting its traditional arts and crafts through institutions like the Hasta Shilpa Vikas Nigam and the Laghu Udyog Vikas Nigam. The government has also successfully engaged the use of technology and design in the traditional skill set for contemporary products, thus expanding the market base. In fact, this dynamism in product diversification has enabled an increase in the export of its handloom and handicraft industry, particularly in the sectors of textile and natural fibres including jute, leather toys and wooden furniture. The field of arts and crafts is further energised by the entry of many new players not only in terms of the expanding number of enterprises, but also by the increased participation of Non-Governmental Organisations (NGOs) who have been particularly active in craft development and outreach at the grass roots level. When civil societies organise social movements, it encourages the formation of self-help groups, who then work together towards creating an alternative and fairer way of doing business.

Because of stiff competition in the global market, there is a pressing need for the state to encourage planning in terms of mapping the traditional wealth of knowledge of raw material and human skill sets, followed by capacity building, design innovation, technology intervention and the protection of intellectual property rights and copyright regulation.

Intellectual Property Rights and their Protection

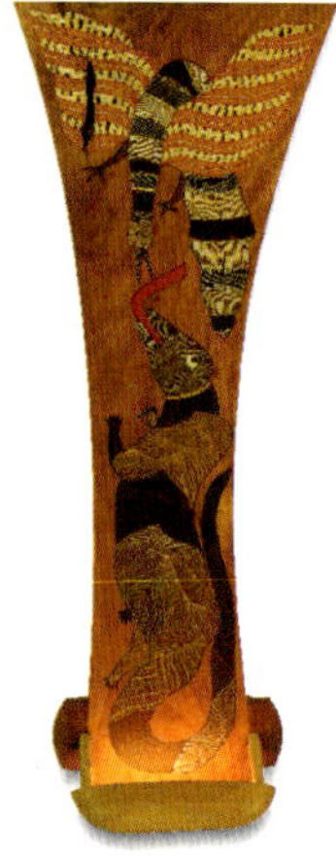

ABOVE
A floor lamp decorated with beautiful Gond art.

The protection of community ownership and traditional knowledge in artisanal clusters is the first and the foremost concern. Once this knowledge and ownership is properly protected, it would form the very basis of restoring dignity to communities, alleviating poverty, and generate sustainable employment opportunities. Crafts are an important part of a country's cultural heritage, and their survival in the midst of strong global market forces requires effective measures to protect the origins of the work, particularly with reference to the communities to which they belong. Possible legal recourse available in India and applicable for protecting arts and crafts as part of traditional knowledge can be handled in several ways.

Protection by means of copyright: These include items embodying a high degree of artistic and creative value, such as jewellery, leather ornaments, etc.

Protection by trademark (collective marks and certification marks): The use of a trademark for a product can be encouraged under this mode and can be developed as a logo and stamped on packaging appropriate for export and for a niche market.

Protection under the Geographical Indications Act: This Act is significant for identifying products with particular geographical origins, like Chanderi or Maheshwari textiles, Bagh block prints, stone carved lattice work of Gwalior, etc. The protection of geographical indications could be combined with the documentation process and for building up heritage items.

Protection by means of patenting: When a craft item has less intrinsic value than the process used to manufacture it, under certain circumstances, a process patent can be filed. It would have to be established that the craftsman has substantially improved an earlier process, inventing an original manufacturing process that is new and suitable for industrial use.

It is rare in the case of craft items. However, different kind of processes involved in carpet-making would fit into this category.

Trade secrets: This is important for those extremely important, unique and significant steps in the process, which are known to only a few critical key actors of the cluster.

Utility models: These are important for that minor inventive step used in a particular artisanal production, which though small is still very crucial to the whole process.

New Management Concepts in Madhya Pradesh

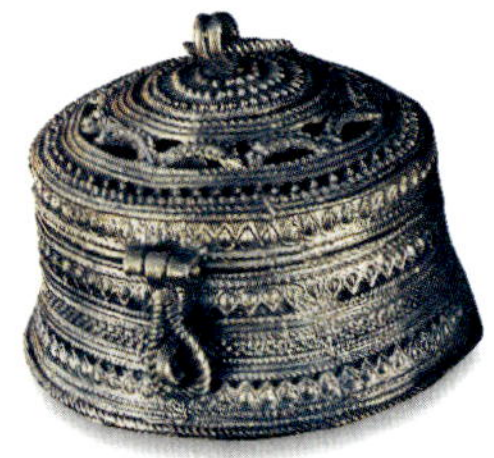

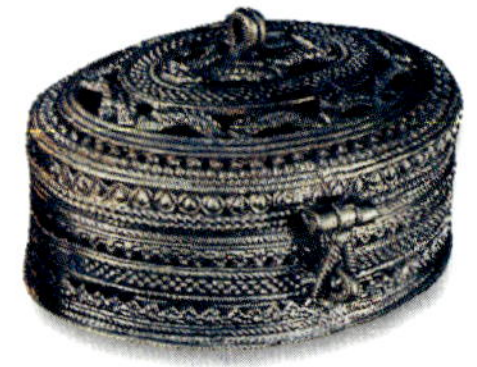

ABOVE
Intricately carved metal boxes from Datia and Tikamgarh.

Marketing traditional crafts as handmade products: Traditional artisanal products continue to have great marketing potential if the market is understood properly. With small changes in terms of design, consumer preference and packaging, these products can be presented as having a unique appeal which sets them apart from the plethora of items traded in the global market. This appeal originates from the very spirit underlying the nature of handmade products, apart from their traditional, religious and social significance. There is an increasing appreciation and attraction amongst consumers the world over for objects fashioned by hand.

The increased role of the Internet: The Internet has become the fastest growing mode of communication and is a useful tool for reaching the market place through advertising and product promotion. Businesses often make use of web technology to make and maintain business contacts, post information on new products, and take orders online. In the arts and crafts sector, web technology will play an increasing role in terms of greater outreach of primary producers like artisans and weavers to the market segment comprising wholesalers, retailers and distributors.

Encouraging innovation: An increasing demand for different products, the influence of using different concepts from craft clusters across the country irrespective of the origin, the increased migration of artisans from different parts of the country, the global demand for new creations along with an increased participation in domestic and international trade fairs have led to the development of 'fusion products' and the discovery of new marketing opportunities. Craftspeople have to continuously innovate and diversify in order to make products relevant to contemporary markets, thereby enhancing employment and livelihood opportunities for local communities. This requires strategic design and technical intervention, training and skill upgradation. It is imperative to build up sectoral capacity and capability in response to challenges, such as the setting up of institutions through education, training, design and other related capacity building programmes.

Encouraging self-help groups: A market driven development of business models for self-help groups, community enterprises, as well as small and medium size enterprises have been encouraged in Madhya Pradesh. Being involved with higher level enterprises encourages organisations at the grass root level to actively participate as shareholders in the trade process.

Increased role of NGOs: NGOs have become the link between formal and informal sectors of the economy. Craftspeople represent an important sector of the economy and the role of NGOs has become important in serving their social and economic interests with regard to unexploitative labour, micro credit access and marketing management along the lines of fair trade.

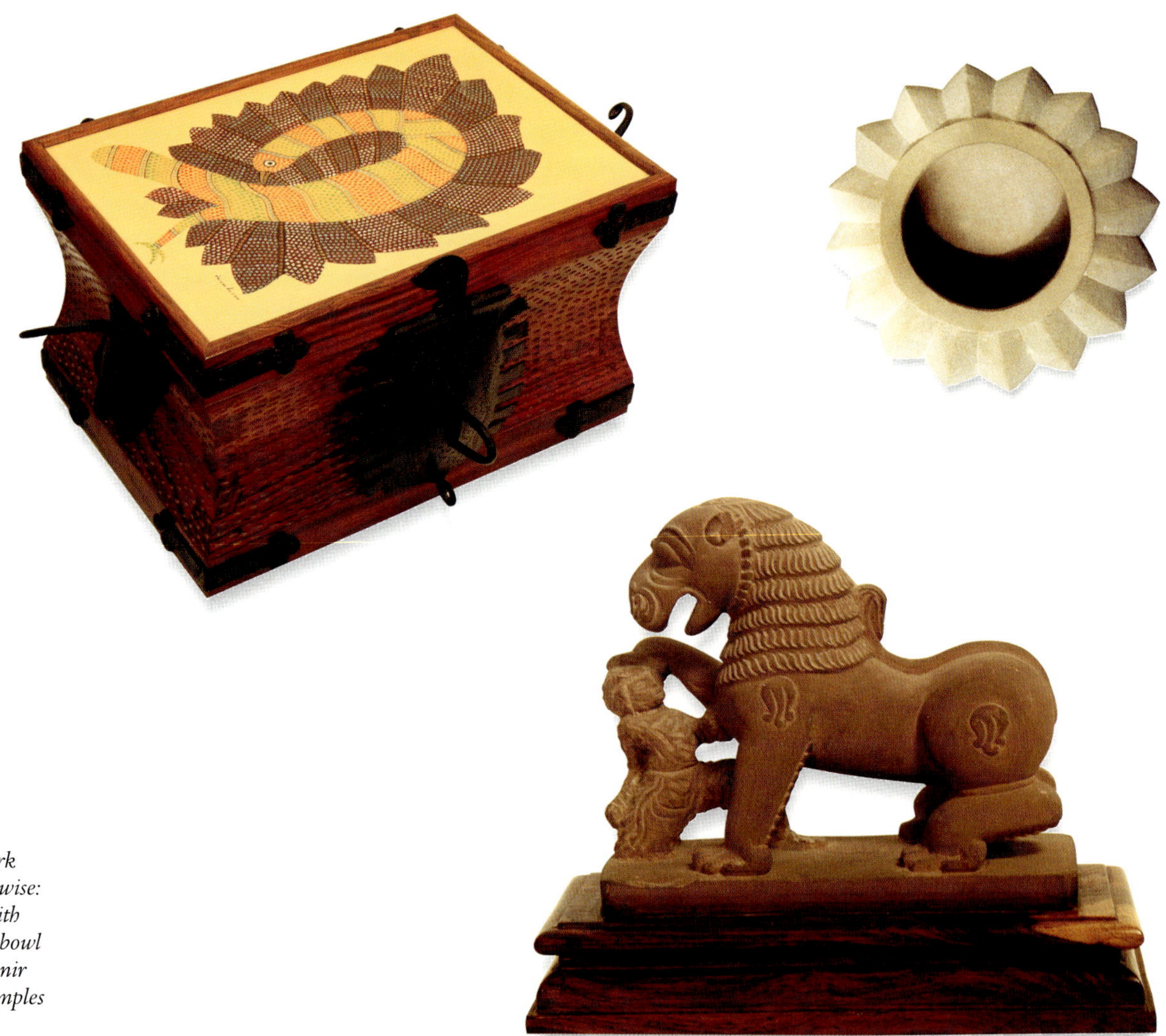

RIGHT
Contemporary products using traditional artwork and motifs. Clockwise: a wooden chest with Gond artwork; a bowl and a stone souvenir inspired by the temples at Khajuraho.

Cluster based craft enterprises: Artisans, weavers and craft enterprises need continuous support in upgrading technical skills, design and managerial inputs in order to sustain themselves in the traditional market, and penetrate new markets. Stiff global competition of the free market economy since the nineties has made these producer groups more vulnerable but at the same time, has also prepared them to continuously innovate with respect to new production techniques and concepts in creativity and design, as well as new modes of management marketing practises.

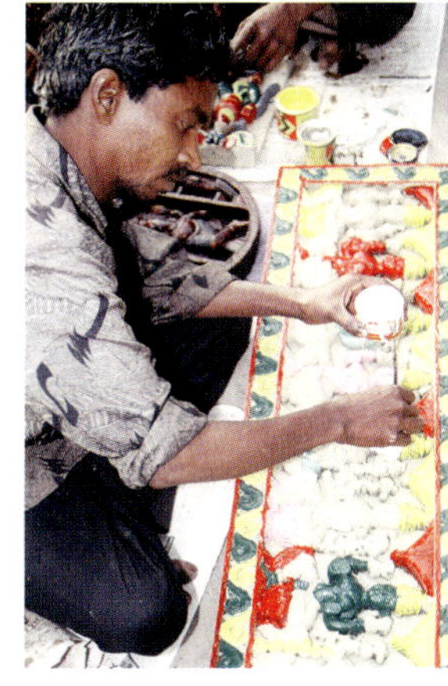

Strengthening institutional capacity: To meet the new challenges of the free market economy, the only way to sustain the artisans lies in capacity building and strengthening institutional capacity to upgrade their skill set. It calls for not only an increased role of the state/public sector, but also the private sector to set up such institutions.

With the setting up of private institutions, such as NIFT in Bhopal, if more branches of reputed national institutions like the National Institute of Design (NID) were to start operating in Madhya Pradesh, these institutions would act as catalysts for change. These institutions endeavour to renew the relevance, the interest and the economic potential of handicrafts and handlooms and other works of arts and crafts through innovation, education, and the enhancement of traditional skills and integrated development. These institutions open up doors for leadership and enterprise building while reviving the pride and value of craft heritage.

ABOVE
A Bhil man painting a wooden sculpture, Jhabua.

Contemporary Products and Indigenous Skills

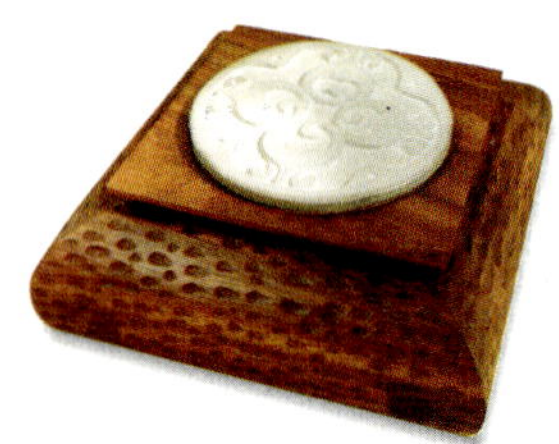

Crafts are a part of our national heritage and are traditionally linked to past and present communities. Arts and crafts have evolved over the years to cater to the demands of the market as part of a contemporary product line. During the last decade, there has been a distinct trend initiated by imaginative designers who believe in the strength of the traditional Indian art form, concept and medium of expression. These designers have infused an intimate knowledge of raw material with design and technology, colour techniques (including the application of natural colours), mainstream architecture and concepts of contemporary products, retaining the natural character of a product through new ways of processing in order to add value in the international market.

Installations like The Seven Steps of Buddha reflect the new trend which is high on retaining the original character of traditional skill sets but yet a new unique product, which can only be a collaborative affair between an artisan and a high level designer and technologist.

ABOVE
A contemporary box made using traditional wood and stone craft.

The process of interaction and dialogue between craftspeople, designers and researchers, as well as an exposure to the outside world, has resulted in creating what could be termed as a new language and expression which is

RIGHT
The Seven Steps of Buddha, a contemporary project, inspired by traditional concepts of design.

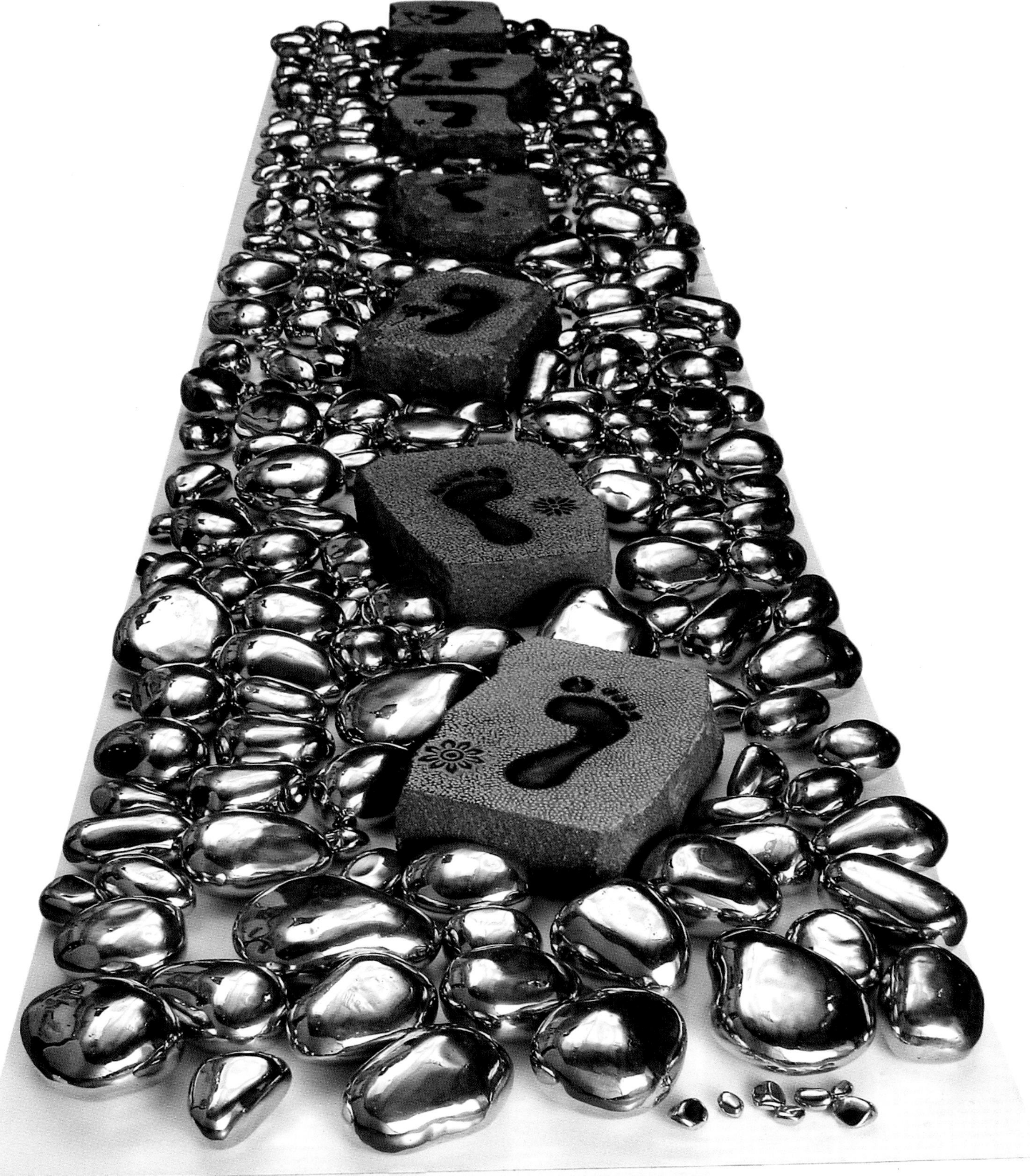

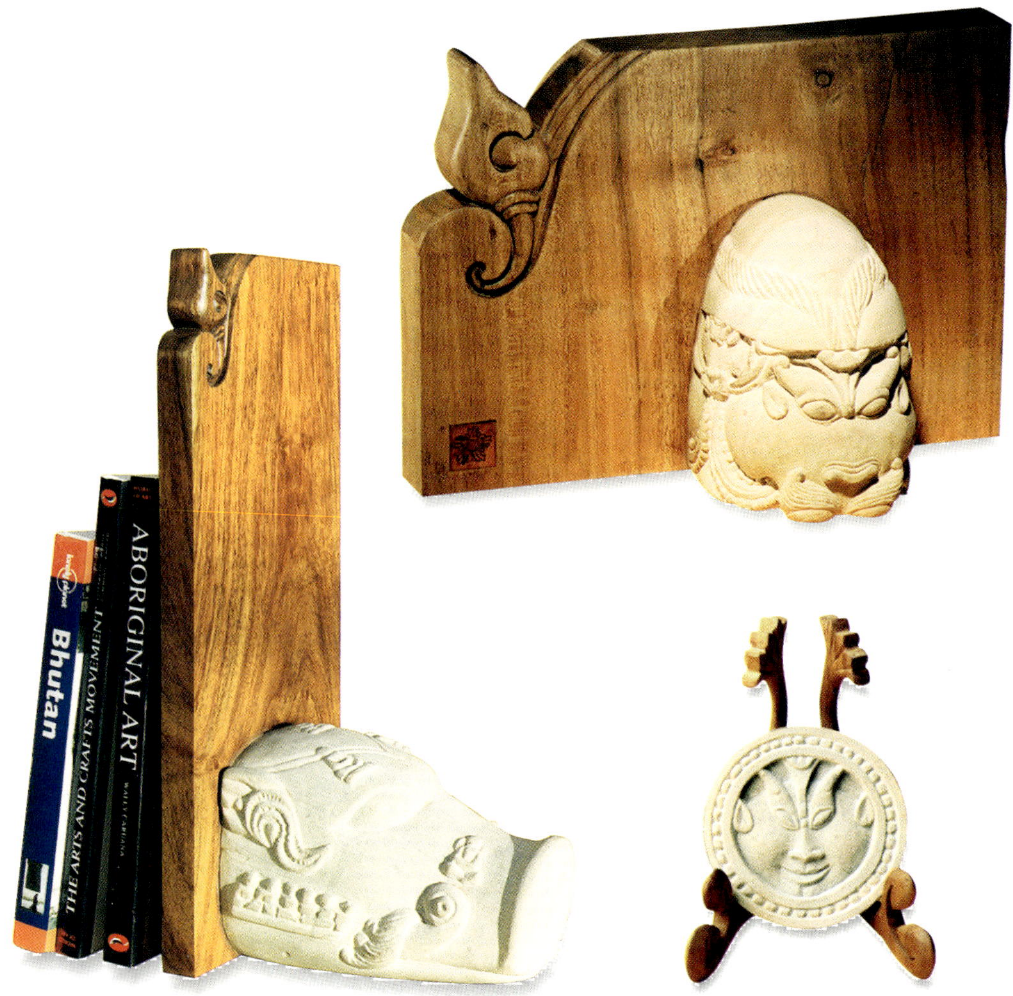

RIGHT
Modern products, like these bookends and plate holder, are inspired by temple motifs.

more enriched but remains pure and fresh. A classic case of this interaction is Bhajju Shyam, hailing from the Mandla region of Madhya Pradesh. He has set a precedent with his three international publications. His first book, brought out by the British Museum in the United Kingdom, is a narrative of his journey, expressed through his paintings, in a unique Mandla Gond style which depicts his experiences in London. The books have been printed in several European languages. The style of painting is a unique way of decorating mud walls in the dwellings of Mandla. This simple form of painting was transformed by the contemporary artist, J. S. Swaminathan, who first took Bhajju's uncle, late Jangarh Singh Shyam, to Bhopal from his remote village. Even though Jangarh died at a young age, his work has found space in many international museums across the world. Realising that it was important for his fellowmen to get a similar kind of exposure, Jangarh encouraged them to travel and experience the outside world. Another example of this process of interaction is the special project commissioned by the Madhya Pradesh Hastshilp Nigam, to Kaaru, a design company. The designers were asked to create a line of souvenirs to commemorate the 'Khajuraho Millennium' celebrations in the year 2001. The designers chose to work with crafts from the state using the many art-forms of the state, ranging from classical to tribal. The designers worked with several artisans to create a wide range of products that were functional and decorative. The designers and artisans spent days observing the ancient temples and deriving motifs and forms that could be translated into products. The product designs then created were specific and unique to the majestic Khajuraho temples.

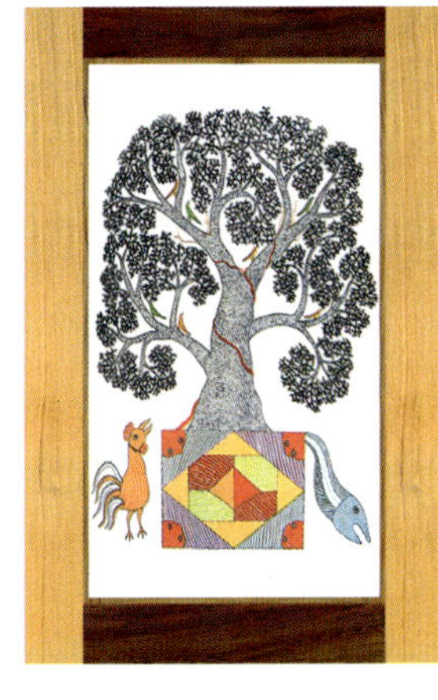

ABOVE
Detail of a painting by Gond tribal artist Bhajju Shyam.

Bamboo Breakthrough

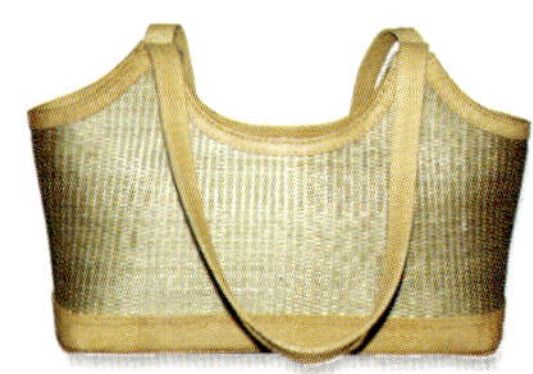

After China, India has the largest bamboo resources in the world. Bamboo fabric was launched during the VII World Bamboo Congress held in New Delhi in 2004. The event has great significance for Madhya Pradesh, since it was with Chanderi that the first experiments of weaving bamboo fibre took place using a mix of bamboo and silk, bamboo and cotton and bamboo and wool.

Bamboo fibre has unparalleled advantages. It is naturally anti bacterial, 100 per cent biodegradable and can be as soft as cashmere. The fabric itself is coarse in texture, but is also very porous. The business from the clothes alone could help capture for India a great chunk of the global $10 billion bamboo market.

Similarly, the use of bamboo for contemporary products such as furniture, toys and other household products has become extremely popular. It is innovations such as these, which not only take into account the natural resources of a region, but also successfully fuse design, durability and aesthetics within environmental parameters, which will herald a new dawn and revival of arts and crafts in Madhya Pradesh.

ABOVE
A modern bamboo shoulder bag.

RIGHT
A woman tends to a young bamboo stalk. Bamboo has been used successfully in Madhya Pradesh to fuse innovation and design.

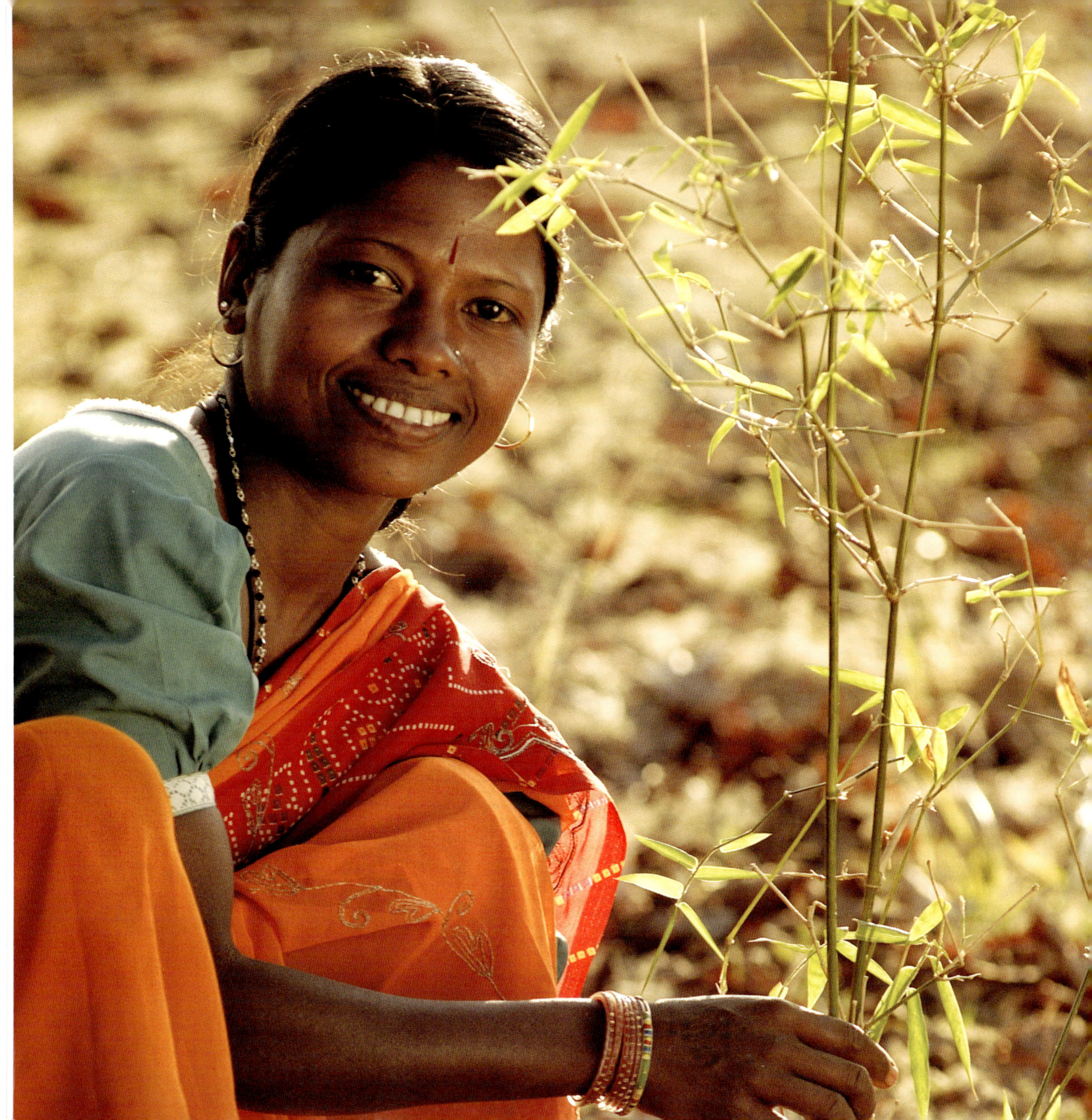

S. No.	Unit	Category	No. of rooms	Tariff (Rs.) Single	Double	Extra Person	Facilities
30	Malwa Retreat (CP) Tel: (07292) 263221 E-mail: mretreatm@mptourism.com	AC Aircooled	2 6	1490 890	1490 890	200 100	
	NEEMUCH						
31	Tourist Motel Tel: (07423) 280080 Email: neemuch@mptourism.com	AC	6	890	890	150	
	OMKARESHWAR						
32	Narmada Resort (CP) Tel: (07280) 271455 E-mail: omkareshwar@mptourism.com	AC Dlx AC Aircooled (budget)	3 8 8	1590 1190 790	1590 1190 790	250 200 100	
	NOWGAON						
33	Highway Treat (CP) Tel: (07685) 256425 E-mail: nowgaon@mptourism.com	Aircooled	2	890	890	150	
	ORCHHA						
34	Betwa Retreat ***(CP) Tel: (07680) 252618, 252402 E-mail: betwa@mptourism.com	Heritage suite (AC) AC AC Tent	1 14 10	4990 1690 1290	4990 1690 1290	700 300 200	
35	Sheesh Mahal (Heritage Hotel)(CP) Telefax: (07680) 252624 E-mail: smorchha@mptourism.com	Maharaja Suite (AC) Maharani Suite (AC) AC AC Single	1 1 5 1	4990 3990 1690 1190	4990 3990 1690 -	700 300 200 -	
	PACHMARHI						
36	Amaltas Tel: (07578) 252098 E-mail: amaltas@mptourism.com	AC Dlx AC	5 5	1890 1590	1890 1590	250 200	
37	Champak Bungalow Tel: (07578) 285315, 285316 E-mail: champak@mptourism.com	AC Dlx AC Tent AC	7 5 7	4190 2790 2790 *(AP rates - inclusive of taxes)*	4690 3290 3290	1090 990 990	
38	Glen View Tel: (07578) 252533, 252445 E-mail: gview@mptourism.com	AC Dlx AC AC Tent	6 15 4	4190 2790 2790 *(AP rates - inclusive of taxes)*	4690 3290 3290	1090 990 990	

S. No.	Unit	Category	No. of rooms	Tariff (Rs.)			Facilities
				Single	Double	Extra Person	
39	Hilltop Bungalow Tel: (07578) 252846 E-mail: hilltop@mptourism.com	AC	5	1890	1890	250	
40	Hotel Highlands Tel: (07578) 252099,252399 E-mail: highland@mptourism.com	AC Aircooled	20 20	1490 990	1490 990	200 200	
41	Panchvati Tel: (07578) 252096 E-mail: panchvati@mptourism.com	Aircooled (cottages) AC (huts)	5 5	1690 1890	1690 1890	250 250	
42	Rock-End Manor Tel: (07578) 252079 E-mail: rem@mptourism.com	AC Dlx	6	4190 *(AP rates - inclusive of taxes)*	4690	1090	
43	Satpura Retreat Tel: (07578) 252097 E-mail: satpura@mptourism.com	AC Dlx AC Standard	2 4	4190 3590 *(AP rates - inclusive of taxes)*	4690 4290	1090 890	
44	Woodland Bungalow (DIB) Tel : (07578) 252272 E-mail: woodlands@mptourism.com	Aircooled	4	990	990	200	
	PENCH						
45	Kipling's Court Tel: (07695) 232830,232850 E-mail: kcpench@mptourism.com	AC Aircooled Dormitory Beds	15 5 10	3240 2290 700 *(AP rates - inclusive of taxes)*	3890 2890 -	800 690 -	
	PIPARIYA						
46	Tourist Motel Tel: (07576) 222299 E-mail: pipariya@mptourism.com	AC	4	890	890	200	
	ROOKHAD						
47	Highway Treat Tel: (07695) 290130 E-mail: rookhad@mptourism.com	Aircooled	4	490	490	100	

S. No.	Unit	Category	No. of rooms	Tariff (Rs.) Single	Double	Extra Person	Facilities
	SANCHI						
48	Gateway Retreat (CP)	AC Dlx	10	1790	1990	300	
	Tel: (07482) 266723	AC	6	1590	1690	300	
	E-mail: grsanchi@mptourism.com	AC (4 bedded)	2	1990	-	-	
		Annexe Dorm Beds	8	200	-	-	
				(No CP rates on dormitory)			
	SATNA						
49	Hotel Bharhut (CP)	AC Dlx	7	2090	2090	300	
	Tel: (07672) 226071, 223223	AC	6	1290	1290	200	
	E-mail: hbsatna@mptourism.com	Aircooled	9	890	890	150	
		Budget Aircooled	4	490	490	100	
	SHIVPURI						
50	Tourist Village*** (CP)	AC	17	1490	1690	200	
	Tel: (07492) 223760, 221297	AC (4 bedded)	2	1890	-	-	
	E-mail: tvshivpuri@mptourism.com						
	TAWA						
51	Tawa Resort	House Boat	2	3990	3990	-	
	Tel: (07572)290337	AC	6	2190	2690	800	
	E-mail: tawa@mptourism.com			*(AP rates - inclusive of taxes)*			
	UJJAIN						
52	Shipra Residency*** (CP)	AC Suite	4	3990	3990	300	
	Tel: (0734) 2551495-96	AC Dlx	3	1690	1690	200	
	3269000, 2552402	AC	21	1290	1290	150	
	E-mail: shipra@mptourism.com						
53	Hotel Avantika (Yatri Niwas)	AC	4	890	890	150	
	Tel: (0734) 2511398	Aircooled	2	690	690	100	
	E-mail: avantika@mptourism.com	(4 bedded)	6	890	890	-	
		Dorm Beds	32	90	-	-